Why is Rita so afraid to trust Mark?

"Rita," Mark called and took hold of her arm.

"I don't want to talk to you right now," Rita repeated. "Don't you understand? You are annoying me with this pressure."

"What are you afraid of?" Mark asked her. He dropped his hand and waited for her reply.

Rita's eyes flashed the warning that her anger had been piqued. "I'm not afraid of anything and I don't owe you any explanations. You've trained me now and I can make the Iditarod a reality without any more interference from you."

"Where is all this fury coming from?" Mark asked. "Is this because I kissed you or because you opened up to me?"

Hitting the raw nerves that made up Rita's emotions, she quickly lowered her head to avoid Mark's reading her eyes. She knew that saying nothing was like surrendering defeat, but in truth she was afraid to say anything. Pushing past him, Rita made her way to the dogs.

Mark stood on the steps watching her walk away. When had he come to care so much about this hurting woman-child? He was almost afraid to search himself for the depth of his concern. What if he learned more than he was willing to deal with?

JANELLE JAMISON is the pen name for Tracie J. Peterson, a very popular inspirational romance writer and regular columnist for a Christian newspaper in Topeka, Kansas.

Books by Janelle Jamison

HEARTSONG PRESENTS

HP19—A Place to Belong
HP40—Perfect Love
HP47—Tender Journeys
HP56—A Light in the Window
HP63—The Willing Heart
HP71—Destiny's Road

Iditarod Dream

Janelle Jamison

The Alaska Trilogy: Book Three

Heartsong Presents

Dedicated to the real Texas Rita and Mark.
Your story is different, but your love is just as real.
I wish for you a life of love for one another and God.

A note from the Author:
I love to hear from my readers! You may correspond with me by writing:

> **Janelle Jamison**
> **Author Relations**
> **P.O. Box 719**
> **Uhrichsville, OH 44683**

ISBN 1-55748-580-1

IDITAROD DREAM

PRINTED IN THE U.S.A.

one

Rita Eriksson shifted into overdrive and watched the highway miles pass by in disinterested silence. Although she'd been away from her childhood home for over five years, the idea of returning held little interest for her.

Born Rita Anne Eriksson, she was the last of ten children and the least cut out for rural life. At least that's what she told herself when she left for college and a degree in nursing.

She'd spent the better part of a lifetime living forty minutes outside the small town of Tok, Alaska. A town seemingly misplaced in the middle of nowhere, between Fairbanks and the Canadian border. It's claim to fame was dog sledding and touristy native art, but to Rita, its only appeal was the fact that the Alcan Highway ran through it. It was on that highway, shortly after she'd finished school, that Rita took off for Anchorage and never looked back.

Ignoring the speed of her car, Rita gave anxious thought to her return home. Most of her brothers and sisters had moved away from Tok, although an older brother and his family had settled in town. Her family was seemingly scattered to the four winds, and for Rita, it was just as well. She'd never fit in with any of them and had come along too late for most of them to even bother being interested in her. Her closest sibling, Edgar, was nearly nine years her senior and, being a boy, he had little interest in the surprise arrival of another sister.

Rita had been only too happy to escape the mundane

lifestyle of a home that until recently, hadn't even afforded them the luxury of electricity or an indoor bathroom. It might not have been so bad had they lived in town. In comparison to the desolation of the Eriksson homestead, there were many things to do in Tok. But Rita had decided to put it all behind her and be done with that way of life.

Yet, even though that had been her choice, here she was driving back home at her parents' urging. Well, not really her parents' urging, more like her father's. She'd always felt closer to her father. For reasons that were beyond Rita's understanding, she and her mother had never gotten along. It seemed that no matter how hard Rita tried, her relationship with her mother only deteriorated to the point that neither of them put much effort into mending the emotional cavern.

Her father, however, loved her and of that Rita was certain. He never failed to call her on Monday nights to find out how her weekend had gone and how the week to come was shaping up. During the entire five years in Anchorage, Rita could remember her mother calling only twice and both those times were on Christmas.

With a shake of her head, Rita tried to ignore the pain she still felt whenever she thought of her mother. There was no sense in letting the past get a stronghold, Rita determined. Nothing was going to change between them. Hadn't time already proved that?

She didn't know how long the flashing red lights of the patrol car had followed her, but when the officer behind the wheel hit the blaring sirens, Rita nearly jumped out of her skin.

"Oh, no!" she muttered and pulled the car to the side of the road. "I wonder how fast I was going?"

She rolled down the window and ran a hand through her

newly cropped black hair. This trip was turning sour rather soon, she thought to herself.

"May I see your driver's license?" a voice called out from overhead.

Rita didn't even bother to look up. She reached over for her red clutch purse and produced her license. Without a word, she handed the license over and then sat tapping her fingers against the steering wheel.

"You were doing eighty-five miles an hour, Ms. Eriksson. Say, you wouldn't be related to August and Beth Eriksson?" the officer questioned.

Rita perked up. Maybe she could beat the ticket if she turned on a little hometown charm.

"Why, yes. They're my parents," she said with a honey smooth voice. Glancing up behind thick black lashes, Rita offered a smile to the stout looking patrolman whose name tag read "Williams."

The officer took off his sunglasses and returned Rita's smile. "Good friends of mine, your folks. I doubt they'd enjoy burying one of their own," he stated evenly. "Being a native, you know better than to drive that fast on this highway. If the road doesn't tear up your vehicle, wrapping it around a moose or grizzly sure could do the job."

"Sorry," Rita said, trying hard to maintain her temper. She didn't appreciate being told what she should and shouldn't do.

"I would hope for at least that much," the officer said as he returned Rita's license with a ticket attached. "I'd let you off with a warning, but being you're a native and not all that sorry, I'd just as soon you learn a lesson."

Rita's temper got the best of her as she snatched the ticket and license from his hand. She thought to say something, but instead stuffed the items inside her purse and turned to roll up her window.

"It was a pleasure meeting you, Ms. Eriksson. I'm sure we'll be seeing more of each other. By the way, I'm Mark Williams."

"It wasn't a pleasure meeting you, Officer Williams and I hope we don't meet again," Rita said curtly and rolled up the car window. She barely waited for the man to walk past her car before hitting the gas and spraying gravel behind her as she pulled back up on the highway.

Rita watched uncomfortably for any sign that the patrol car intended to follow her. When it remained in place at the side of the highway, she breathed a sigh of relief and glanced at her watch.

She'd already been driving for four hours without stopping to get out and stretch and her legs and some other body parts were beginning to ache.

She calculated that her destination was still another hour away. Making mental note of the scenery and the mile markers, Rita realized there wouldn't be much in the way of places to take a break and when the first available turn off the highway presented itself, she took it.

Bouncing down the dusty gravel road, Rita found herself coming to a stop when the road dead ended. Grimacing, Rita walked several yards into the trees and decided to walk a little farther and stretch her legs.

Tall, black spruce rose up in contrast against the long, white trunks of birch trees, while the lavender petals of fireweed waved welcomes from their red stems.

Rita pushed on through the trees and underbrush, enjoying the walk in spite of herself. Something about the area seemed more than just vaguely familiar and, when the trees gave way to a small lake, Rita recognized the place as one she and her father had dog sledded to on many occasions.

The very thought of dog sledding caused Rita to smile. If the truth were known, it was the main reason she'd allowed her father to talk her into coming back home for a visit. He was trying to help her dream of racing in the Iditarod come true.

The Iditarod! A dog sled race to equal no other and Rita was determined to one day be a part of it. She still remembered stories her father had told her about the old dog sled mail trails. Moonlit nights on the trail, the icy winds, and the solitude of having nothing and no one but yourself and the dogs against the elements. It thrilled Rita like nothing else and she wouldn't be complete until she'd experienced "The Last Great Race."

"Ooof!"

The sound caused the hair to prickle on the back of Rita's neck. Snapping her head up, she searched the area for the unmistakable sound of a disturbed bear.

No more than twenty feet away, a mother grizzly woofed a command to her cub before striking a protective stance between Rita and her young.

Rita knew better than to run or cry. Bears seemed more inclined to attack humans when they made noises similar to animals in distress. August had told his daughter on more than one occasion to stand her ground silently and only as a last resort should she curl up into a ball and play dead.

Rita shoved her hands into the pockets of her fleece-lined sweat top and made eye contact with the grizzly. The bear took a step forward and made a grunting woof.

Rita could feel her legs trembling beneath her jeans. She knew she was in grave danger, but there was nothing to do but wait out the situation. Somewhere to her left, Rita heard a rustling in the brush. Would it be another bear? Perhaps the cub had somehow gotten behind her.

The bear advanced another two steps at the same time Mark Williams emerged from the trees. Rita's relief was short lived, however, as the mother bear let out a roar.

"Don't move," Mark said in a hushed tone.

"Don't worry," Rita breathed, "I won't."

Rita struggled to keep from going back on her word. Her fear told her to run, and yet her mind rationalized that it would be exactly the wrong thing to do.

"Give her your jacket," Mark suggested.

"What?" Rita questioned in a whisper.

"Take off your jacket and toss it on the ground. Move real slow and don't throw it at her, just over in that direction," Mark said while slowly pulling his revolver from its holster.

Rita slowly pulled her hands from her pockets. "But, it's not a jacket," Rita argued under her breath.

"I don't care if it's a ball gown. Just give it to her and maybe she'll be satisfied enough to let you back away. If not," Mark leveled the .44 magnum in the direction of the bear, "I'll shoot and you back away."

Rita contemplated his words for only a moment before reaching up to undo the zipper. Making deliberate, slow moves, Rita eased out of her top and tossed it to the side of the grizzly.

"Now, move away," Mark said as he put himself between Rita and the bear.

The bear grunted and stomped at her shirt while Rita and Mark backed away. The bear clamped mighty jaws around the fabric of Rita's top and trotted off in the direction the cub had disappeared. When she was out of sight, Mark stopped and put a hand on Rita's arm.

"Are you all right?" he questioned.

Rita suddenly became conscious of being cold, wearing a

cotton tee shirt.

Mark tried to hide a grin while he eased out of his jacket. "Here, I wouldn't want you to catch a chill."

Rita couldn't bear the humiliation and grabbed the jacket without a word. She pulled it on while walking back to her car.

"I have more clothes in the car," she called over her shoulder. "I'll give this back to you in a minute."

"What, no thanks?" Mark questioned in a teasing tone.

Rita refused to give in to his bantering. "I was doing okay," she said, fumbling in her jeans for her car keys.

"Oh, yeah, I could see that," Mark replied sarcastically.

Rita opened the trunk and pulled out a suitcase. Grabbing the first thing she could find, Rita produced an ecru-colored sweater, which she put on.

"There," Rita said as she threw the jacket against Mark's back. "Now that you've done your good deed for the day you can go."

Mark turned around and picked up his patrol jacket. "Is there some reason you can't be civil?" His tone of voice told Rita he wasn't kidding.

She stared for a moment at the brown-haired man. His dark eyes seemed to pierce her conscience. "Sorry," she offered by way of an apology.

"Well, that's at least civil," Mark said as he pulled his jacket back on. "Look, I'm mighty fond of your father and mother, and I know it'd pretty much break their hearts if you were to get yourself killed."

"Don't worry about it," Rita said, reverting to her anger. "I don't."

"What's with you?" Mark questioned the angry, petite woman.

"I don't see that my private life is any of your business.

This whole situation has been more than a little embarrassing and now if you'll excuse me, I'm expected at home,"
Rita stormed the words and climbed into her car.

"Don't speed," Mark said with a grin.

Rita felt more frustration than she was willing to put into
words. She flashed her dark eyes at Mark. "Like I said,
don't worry about it. I'm a big girl."

"I'm well aware of that Ms. Eriksson," Mark offered with
a chuckle. "I'm very well aware of that."

two

"We're mighty glad to see you home safe," August Eriksson said, embracing Rita.

Rita nearly fell into her father's arms. How she longed for a human touch, although she would have never admitted it. "It's good to see you, Dad," Rita whispered against his ear. She pulled back and scrutinized the man before her. He seemed so much older than she remembered. His hair was snowy white and his face much more wrinkled and worn.

Beth Eriksson emerged from the kitchen to appraise the scene. "Hello, Rita," she offered with a smile. "Good to have you back."

"Thanks, Mom," Rita replied and went to where her mother stood. The embrace they shared wasn't the same as the one Rita had just given her father. It was curt, almost a polite symbolic gesture.

"Are you hungry?" Beth asked her daughter.

"Starved and then some," Rita answered with a laugh. "I didn't plan on taking so long to get here."

"Well, I have some sandwich makings in the kitchen. Why don't you just leave your things until after you eat. Then you can get settled in your old room," her mother said in an unemotional way. From the tone set between mother and daughter, it would have been impossible to tell that they were anything more than acquaintances. And, in Rita's mind, they were merely that and little more.

Rita followed her mother and father into the kitchen. They

seemed as happy with one another as they had when she was a child. Her father still looked at her mother with a glow of admiration in his eyes. What was it that he saw in her that merited such praise?

Rita sat politely listening as her parents filled her in on the community and all that had happened in five years. She hung on her father's every word, while barely commenting on her mother's information regarding the family.

"And so, have you considered what I suggested?" August asked.

"And what was that, dear?" Beth asked with a note of surprise in her voice.

"I suggested that our daughter take time off before joining the work force grind, and race the Iditarod next year," August answered his wife.

Beth's face masked any reaction she had to August's words and instead she simply replied, "How interesting."

Rita wondered how her mother really felt about the matter. Would she resent her youngest daughter's presence in the big, rambling log home?

"I have been thinking about it," Rita admitted. "I know the opportunity is one that will probably never come again."

"That's why you should jump at the chance," her father remarked.

"I'm so out of shape though. What with all my studies and work at the hospital, I haven't been outdoors long enough to walk around the block. I can only imagine what it would be like to run with a dog sled team," Rita replied, taking the plate her mother offered. Despite their differences, Rita noted that her mother had made her favorite roast beef sandwich.

"Thanks, Mom," Rita added and offered her mother a hint of a smile.

"But all of that will come back to you. You can start this summer and run with the dogs. You can spend all fall and winter on the trails around here, maybe even run in another race or two just to get primed for the big one," August said in a way that almost sounded as though he were begging.

"And you really think I'd be able to do it?" Rita asked, hopefully. "You think I could manage it all? All the training and getting into shape?"

"You're no Eriksson if you can't!" August exclaimed good-naturedly. "Besides, you'll have nine months to do it in. I've got plenty of good dogs and there's a friend or two in the area that would be happy to have you along on practice runs."

"What do you mean? You'd be handling my training, wouldn't you?" Rita inquired.

"Now, Rita, I'm not the young man I used to be. I can't handle the trails like before. I'll take care of things around here, but when you start practicing on the rougher trails, you'll have to do it without me," August answered.

"But being with you was the biggest reason I was considering it," Rita said in a pouting tone.

"Rita," Beth said a little harsher than she'd intended, "your father is entitled to take care of himself. I need him as much as you do."

Rita turned to face her mother for a moment. There was no need in sharing their differences only twenty minutes into their visit. "I understand that, Mother. I guess if I do it, I'll just run alone."

"There's really no need to do that. Like I said, I have a couple of trusted friends in the area and you could learn a lot from them. Especially where the newer techniques come into play. Both of them even raced in the Iditarod last year. They know a whole heap more about what to expect than I do. You know very well that my only attempt was several years ago and I didn't even finish the race."

"Yes, but you won the silver ingots for being the first to reach the halfway point," Rita offered as consolation.

"I know, but I dropped out shortly after that and these men have both completed the race. Besides, I trust them completely and I know you'd like them. They'd make interesting company and maybe you'd even find yourself fancying one of them. They're both single."

"Oh, Dad," Rita moaned and rolled her eyes. "I'm certainly not up here to husband hunt."

"Then what are you up here for? You haven't seen us in over five years and yet I know that it wasn't for the joy of seeing us that you came home. You want that race. You've always wanted it. Are you going to throw away the only chance you may ever have to race the Iditarod? Are you going to give up your dream?" August asked seriously.

Rita contemplated her father's words for a moment. She was grateful that her mother remained silent. Her father was perfectly right about the conditions being too hard for him. He wasn't young anymore and yet, Rita really needed him to be.

"All right," Rita finally spoke. "I'll go for it. I'll do it your way and I'll finish the race for both of us!"

"Good girl," August said, slamming his hands down on the table. "By next March you'll be able to run with the pros and I'll expect a healthy finish."

"What? You don't demand that I win?" Rita said with a laugh.

"No, it'll be enough just to see you run it and do your best," August replied with pride beaming in his eyes. None of his other children had taken the interest in dog sledding that Rita had, and he was excited about her decision.

Rita turned to her mother. Beth sat quietly eating her sandwich, her face void of anything that would signal to Rita what she thought of the plan.

"Will it be all right with you, Mom?" Rita dared the question.

Beth looked surprised that Rita would consult her about her feelings on the matter. "I support whatever your father wants, Rita. I, too, hope to see you accomplish your dream. It won't be an easy task, but then good things seldom come free of strife."

Rita nodded. "I guess when I'm done here, I'll unpack my things. Then you can tell me where we go from there, Dad."

"Oh, I nearly forgot," August remarked with a quick glance at his wife, "we've planned a bit of a homecoming party for you."

"I wish you hadn't," Rita said with noted frustration in her voice. "You know how I hate parties."

"That's what I told him, but he insisted," Beth offered.

"Well," August continued, "it's just a small get-together. Old friends, new friends, maybe even some family. Tonight at seven, and I promise not to throw another one without consulting you first." His eyes betrayed the anticipation of showing his youngest daughter off, and so Rita agreed without fuss.

I only have to get through this evening, Rita thought as she ate her sandwich, after that everything else will be simple.

❧

Rita tried on three outfits before finally settling on a calf-length denim skirt and light-blue cashmere sweater. She was finishing dressing by pulling on high, black boots when a knock sounded at the door.

"It's open," Rita called out as she finished with her boots.

"Are you nearly ready?" Beth asked her daughter. She noted how graceful Rita looked as she crossed the room and ran a brush through her short, dark hair. She was so much like her father.

"Just finishing up," Rita replied over her shoulder. "I couldn't decide what to wear."

"You look fine," Beth offered, hoping that it wouldn't offend Rita. Sometimes the strangest things seemed to set her daughter off.

"You really think so?" Rita asked, running a hand down her skirt. "Everything seemed wrinkled."

"It looks nice, Rita. Your father is really anxious to show you off, and since most everyone is already here, I thought I'd escort you. That is, if you don't mind," Beth stated hopefully.

Rita was surprised at her mother's gesture, but refused to show it. "It sounds fine, Mom," she said, following her mother into the hall.

Descending the stairs, Rita could hear the soft, classical music her mother had put on the stereo. Mozart. No, Chopin, Rita decided. It sounded nice, and Rita turned to tell Beth so, but found her mother's attention already directed to the crowd as they stepped into the vestibule.

"Beth, don't you look pretty," an older man said as he stepped forward and kissed Rita's mother on the cheek.

"You're kind to say so, Ernie, but I think you'd best have the eye doctor check out your vision," Beth replied and Ernie laughed. "Rita, you remember Ernie, don't you?"

"Of course," Rita said and smiled sweetly.

"Well, don't be telling me this is the baby of the family," Ernie replied, giving Rita a hearty squeeze. "It don't seem possible."

"I know what you mean," August said as he came up from behind Beth. "Rita's become a nurse just like her Aunt Julie. I can't believe a person could change so much in just five years."

"I grew up, Daddy," Rita offered. "That's all. Are you still in the kennel business, Ernie?" Rita hoped her question would take the focus off of herself. She remembered Ernie loved to talk about his dogs.

"Naw, gave it up about a year ago. Got to be too much work for just me," Ernie replied.

"Boy, that's the truth," August said, sounding tired. "That's why I got a partner. None of the kids seemed interested in joining me, so it seemed the logical thing to do."

"A partner?" Rita questioned her father in surprise. "When did you get a partner?"

August chuckled at Rita's reaction. "I guess I forgot to tell you about that. I'll introduce you to him tonight. He's a real nice guy, and one of those fellows I was telling you about earlier."

Rita bit back a response as her mother pulled her along and into a sea of people. "I thought you said this was a small get-together," Rita commented.

"To your father, this is a small get-together," Beth reminded her daughter.

Rita nodded, knowing how her father loved to keep friends and family close at hand. He was always inviting someone over for some reason.

"Rita!" a woman's voice exclaimed.

Rita looked up to find an old high school friend. "Janice?" She barely resembled the girl Rita had known. Her once long blond hair was cut short, and her figure was generously rounded in the expectation of a new child.

"It's really me," the woman replied. "I can't believe

you're finally here. You will come over to spend some time with me and Dave, won't you?"

"Of course," Rita said, still stunned by her friend's appearance.

"We're living in Tok, same old place, so just make your way on over whenever you can. But I warn you, the place is a mess what with the kids and all," Janice said with a laugh.

"Kids? I thought maybe this was your first one," Rita said, indicating Janice's condition.

"Oh, no. This is number five," Janice replied.

"Five?" Rita questioned. She could see that Janice was radiant and happy and knew there wasn't any sense in spoiling it with lectures of world conditions and such. "How nice," Rita added instead and left the woman with promises to visit.

She made the rounds bidding "hellos" to all the neighbors and church friends that she'd known. That life seemed a million years ago, however, and Rita felt rather out of place. So many of these people had drifted out of her thoughts and heart and now she felt hesitant to allow them back in.

Independence had made Rita hard. She knew it and she actually found herself supporting the role. Being aloof and indifferent left her more time to herself and with more control in her life.

She was just trying to figure a way out of the room, when August called from the doorway. "Rita, come meet my partner."

Rita made her way through the crowd of well-wishers and glanced up in time to come face-to-face with Mark Williams.

"Rita, this is Mark Williams, my partner," August stated. "Mark, my youngest daughter, Rita."

Mark grinned from ear to ear and extended his hand. "Rita, it's a pleasure."

"I don't believe this," Rita said, refusing Mark's hand and turning to her father. "He's your partner?"

"Do you two know each other?" August asked, looking curiously from Mark to Rita.

"You'll have to excuse me," Rita said, and hurried from the room.

She hated herself for the way she'd responded to Mark's presence, but she couldn't imagine anything more embarrassing than having to face Mark Williams again. Making her way through the kitchen and out the back door, Rita didn't stop moving until she was well behind the house and halfway to the creek that ran the full length of the property.

"I don't believe it," she sighed aloud. "It's bad enough Dad's taken on a partner, but why did it have to be him?"

The breeze picked up, chilling Rita momentarily. She hugged her arms to her chest and gazed up into the sky.

"You really should learn to layer your clothes," Mark teased.

Rita snapped around to find him not two feet from where she stood. "Haven't you put me through enough? First you give me a speeding ticket, then you make me give up my clothes to a bear, and now I learn that I must endure your company for the months to come if I'm to get the training I need for the Iditarod."

"In the first place, you deserved the speeding ticket," Mark said with a shrug. "Now, are you going to dispute that?"

"No, I suppose not," Rita muttered.

"And secondly, as embarrassing as it was, giving your top to that grizzly got her attention on something other than you, and finally, I told you that your folks and I were good friends," Mark stated firmly.

"Good friends are one thing. Partners are entirely something else. I had no idea my father had even taken on a partner, much less that it was you," Rita said, and turned to walk away.

"I wish for the sake of your father and mother, you'd just drop what's gone behind us. I'd like to start over," Mark said, following Rita back to the house.

Rita stopped and turned to face the man who'd caused her nothing but embarrassment and grief. "Look, for my father's sake I will act civilly and cooperate. But, and this is most important," Rita said with determination, "I don't need you or anyone else telling me how to live my life. I can take care of myself, just as I have for the last five years. I came here to train for the Iditarod, not to make friends or hunt for a husband, as my father would like me to do."

"I can't imagine wanting to be either one," Mark replied sarcastically and left Rita to stare open-mouthed after him.

three

At breakfast the following morning, Rita was still thinking about Mark's words. She wasn't sure why it should bother her so much, but it did.

He had no right to talk to me that way, Rita thought. She shoveled scrambled eggs and toast into her mouth without even tasting the food.

"You're kind of preoccupied this morning, aren't you?" August asked his daughter and took a seat beside her.

"Sorry," Rita offered, wiping toast crumbs from her tee shirt. "I just keep thinking about all the work I need to do." It wasn't a lie, Rita decided. She really had been thinking of a variety of things, it was just that Mark Williams seemed to take up most of her attention.

"Well, I think the first thing we do should be to reacquaint you with the dogs. There's a few of the older ones we use for breeding who'll remember you, but the dogs you'll need to use for the race will be the three- and four-year-old ones."

"I thought of that," Rita said, sipping hot coffee. "I can do the feeding and care for the ones you pick out."

"We'll work together to pick out twenty or thirty that look like good possibilities for the race. You can work with those dogs on a daily basis," August stated. "We can choose them after breakfast, if that's all right with you."

"Sounds good to me," Rita replied. She looked forward to working with her father and, in spite of her worries about his health and age, Rita knew the kennel was his domain.

❧

Half an hour later, Rita followed her father from dog to dog. The Eriksson kennel had over one hundred dogs; far more animals than had been there before Rita had gone to Anchorage. It was easy to see why August needed a partner.

After only ten minutes of listening to her father point out the virtues of one dog after the other, Rita was annoyed to find herself having to deal with Mark again.

"Good morning," Mark said as he passed by with a bag of feed hoisted over his shoulder.

"It was," Rita muttered and turned to her father. "What's he doing here?"

"I told you. He's my partner. One hundred and ten dogs need a lot of attention. We work at this thing on a constant basis," August replied.

"But I thought he was a cop," Rita said without thinking her father might wonder how she knew that detail of Mark's life.

"Oh that," August said with a shrug. "He just fills in on the weekends. Most of the time he's here with me."

"Great," Rita stated sarcastically and walked away to look at the dogs on her own.

"There's a lot of anger in that woman," Mark stated, putting the feed on the ground beside him. He pulled out a ball cap from his back pocket and secured it on his head.

"I know," August replied. He watched as Rita moved from dog to dog. She'd always gotten along better with animals than people, August reminded himself. It wouldn't have been all that surprising had she handled Mark with cool indifference, but her hateful attitude seemed out of place, even for Rita.

August turned to Mark. "What happened between you two? She has a real mean streak for you."

Mark chuckled and relayed his first and second meeting with Rita. He finished up by telling August about their conversation the night of the party.

"I guess she thought she was losing control of the situation. Control has always been a big issue with Rita." August's words caused Mark to sober considerably.

"She won't have as much control out there on the trails. The weather, the wildlife, all of it has a mind of its own," Mark stated as if August didn't already know it.

"Rita's always cherished independence," August replied. He was still watching Rita and knew she was trying not to notice Mark and August as they talked. "Since she was a little girl, Rita has alienated herself from just about everything, for fear it might require she give up some form of control in her life. Didn't matter what or who it was. She put up a wall between herself and her mother, God, teachers, friends, and sometimes even me."

"I wonder why she feels so insecure?" Mark questioned.

"Insecure? I've thought of Rita as a lot of things but never insecure. Why, she trekked out of here on her own as fast as her car could take her. Of course you know how she is behind the wheel," August added with a laugh.

Mark smiled, but he challenged August's words. "Rita strikes me as the type of person who's never found her niche. She seems out of place and I think she purposefully makes it that way in order that no one and nothing gets too close. I think she's insecure about forming relationships. Maybe she's afraid that the feelings she puts out won't be reciprocated."

"I suppose that's a possibility. I just never thought about

it. Now that I do, it seems to make some sense. I just always thought she was spoiled and headstrong."

"Oh she is that, August," Mark agreed. "But I don't think it's the reason she distances herself. No, I think Rita's been hurt by someone, and she's not about to let anyone have the chance to let her down again."

August grimaced at Mark's words. He knew only too well of the soured relationship between Rita and Beth. Rita had turned away from her mother at a very early age, but for what reason, August was never sure. Beth had never wanted to discuss it, and Rita claimed to never understand it. August had been forced to stand by helplessly while the relationship deteriorated at a rapid pace.

"Dad!" Rita called from the dogs. "Is this dog one of Blueberry's pups?"

August smiled. Blueberry had been Rita's favorite pet before she'd left for Anchorage. "You've got a good eye, Rita. That's Dandelion, so named because he used to chew on them all the time. He's a good runner and one of the very dogs I thought you could use."

Rita ran her hand over the husky's backside. "He feels real firm," she replied.

"And he's a great leader," Mark added. He and August walked to where Rita continued to check him out. "I've run him in lead just about every time I've had him out. He seems to get out of sorts if you do otherwise."

"I know the feeling," Rita muttered under her breath. Mark caught the words but said nothing.

"Look, Rita," August began, "I want you and Mark to work well together. Do you suppose you could put whatever is bothering you aside and just try to make the relationship work?"

Rita's head snapped up. She bit off a rhetorical reply when she saw the pleading in her father's eyes. He was the only man for which she'd even consider backing away from a fight.

Mark noticed the change in Rita's facial expression as she caught sight of her father. She truly loved the man, which gave Mark hope. At least she was capable of love. Now, why did that matter? Mark tossed the thought from his mind and waited for Rita to make some formal statement of peace.

Rita struggled for the right words. She didn't like giving in or letting Mark win, but for some reason it was important to her father and that made it important to her. "I'm sorry, Mark," Rita finally said, turning to face her adversary. "I guess I got carried away with my anger. Truce?"

"Truce," Mark said and offered his hand.

Rita reached out and took Mark's hand. She was instantly aware of the way his big hand engulfed her smaller one. It was difficult to allow the contact and yet almost pleasant the way he squeezed her hand and smiled.

Rita quickly dropped his hand, confused by the feelings Mark had stirred. "So what dogs do you recommend, Mark?" she quickly asked to cover up her feelings.

By late in the afternoon, Mark, Rita, and August had picked twenty-two dogs that seemed to fit the description of what Rita needed. These dogs had endurance and youth, experience and grace. They were a sturdy breed of husky, with crystal blue eyes and stout, firm bodies.

Rita worked with the men to relocate the dogs. They moved dog houses, straw, stake-out chains, and dogs, until Beth called them for supper.

"Have dinner with us, Mark," August said, walking with Rita to the outdoor pump.

"Naw," Mark said, pulling off the ball cap and stuffing it

into his back pocket again. "I've got things to take care of at home. Besides, I threw a roast in the crockpot before I left this morning."

Rita was relieved at Mark's reply, but said nothing. She pushed and pulled at the pump handle until icy water flowed in a steady stream. Washing her hands and face with the strong, disinfectant soap that was left on a metal stand beside the pump, Rita felt refreshed and famished.

*

The days that followed found Rita in a constant state of retraining. Things she'd learned as a child had to be reviewed, while new ideas and techniques were introduced.

Rita had taken to jogging with Dandelion, whom she immediately dubbed "Dandy." She wanted to establish a strong relationship with the dog before working with the others. If the leader and driver were to work as one, they had to know each other intimately.

Rita enjoyed the playful dog. He was easy to love and filled a void in Rita's heart. No wonder she'd always found the dogs such pleasant company. They didn't ask about your feelings but simply accepted whatever you were capable of giving.

One crisp morning as she finished her run with Dandy, Rita was surprised when Mark appeared on the gravel road astride a motorcycle.

"Morning," he called out as he came up alongside Rita and Dandy.

"Hi," Rita said and slowed to a rapid walk.

"Want a ride back?" Mark offered.

"No, I'm fine," Rita replied, trying to soften the severity of her tone. "I need to walk. I still have flappy legs and no muscle tone."

"You look pretty good to me," Mark said with a grin.

Rita blushed and tried to ignore the fact that Mark noticed her discomfort with a broader smile.

"Dad tells me that you're going to race in the Iditarod," Rita said, hoping to steer the conversation away from herself.

"That's right," Mark replied, keeping even pace with Rita. "I wouldn't miss it. Last year I came in high enough to make money on it. I intend to win it this year."

"Oh, really?" Rita said as her eyes met Mark's.

"Do I denote a bit of challenge in that question?" Mark asked.

"You might," Rita said, enjoying the banter.

"You realize the odds are against you. Few women even race the Iditarod, much less win it. Besides, I'm more experienced than you and you have flappy legs. Remember?" Mark's amusement was contagious.

Rita smiled in spite of her resolve to be serious. "I thought you said they looked pretty good," Rita answered.

"They do, but not for dog sledding. I think they'd look great beneath the hem of a skirt while accompanying me to dinner." Mark's statement was a clear invitation.

Rita shook her head. "I'm not about to fraternize with the competition," she replied. "You might learn all my strategies, and then I'd lose the race to you."

"You will anyway," Mark said with a laugh. "And I already know all your strategies. I'm the teacher, remember?"

Rita tossed her head and ignored the laughing man at her side. She didn't like the way he made her feel. She was afraid of feeling too much for him and determined within herself to avoid a deeper relationship than that of student and teacher.

⋇

Later that night, Rita took a quiet moment for herself and walked down to see her dogs. They were a good bunch. Dandy was white and tawny brown with streaks of black. Muffin was black and white, while Raven was so named for her coal black coat. Toby and Teddy were matched with white blazes against silver and black fur and the others were a hodgepodge of black, brown, and white.

"There isn't a bad one in the lot," August stated, breaking Rita's solitude.

"I was just thinking that myself," Rita responded. "I want very much to know them all at once, and yet I know there's plenty of time."

"It might be a good idea to start hitching them up to the four-wheeler. You could run them up and down the road like Mark does with the others," August suggested.

"All right, but I doubt I'll be any good at it. It's been so long since I've even hitched a team. I've probably forgotten all about it," Rita answered.

"Don't worry about it, Rita. You'll do just fine and if you need anything, Mark and I will be here to help."

Rita nodded and braved the question she'd been wanting to ask. "Why Mark? For a partner I mean. Where's he from and why did you pick him?"

"I met him at church the summer you left home. He seemed like a good man. He had a great love of animals and from the start all he ever talked about was raising a sled team. I offered to help him. We've been working together ever since," August replied.

"I didn't realize you'd had a partner that long."

"I haven't. I just made him a partner last fall. He's a

good, Christian man, Rita. I hope you'll give him a chance. I believe he was an answer to my prayers and your mother's," August stated, even knowing that Rita thought very little about the power of prayer.

"I didn't even know you were looking for a partner," Rita said, trying not to sound too disappointed that her father hadn't confided in her.

"I guess I just started showing my age. The mornings got to be such a chore that all I wanted to do was stay in bed. I gave serious thought to getting rid of the dogs altogether, but I kept hoping you'd come home and fulfill your dream. So I hung on," August replied and added, "I suppose after you're gone, I'll sell out to Mark and let him take it all."

Rita fought back a sadness that threatened to materialize into tears. If her father was getting rid of the dogs, he must feel that his life was coming to an end. The dogs were everything to him, and Rita knew that August wouldn't part with them otherwise.

"Look," August said, noting Rita's sudden quietness, "God will take care of me, just as He always has. You'd do well to remember that and give it a little thought for yourself. You know I don't like to preach at you, but things haven't changed. I still worry about you, and I worry about your soul."

Rita hurried to embrace her father. "Don't worry about me, Daddy. I'm strong and quite capable of taking care of myself. You do what you have to, but don't worry about me."

Rita couldn't bring herself to admonish him for his reminder that she was still walking outside of God's truth. She was informed more often than not, by her mother, that she was the only one of the Eriksson children not to have made a decision for the Lord. It seemed to hang on Beth like a griev-ous weight.

Maybe that was why Rita clung stubbornly to her own nature. She refused to allow herself to think on the matter any further. God was only a tiny part of her worries. Mark Williams was quite another matter.

four

Rita couldn't believe how quickly the summer passed. Before she knew it, the first heavy frost was upon the land leaving an icy signature on the once-green valleys. The air was noticeably colder, and every morning Rita saw subtle changes that pointed clearly to the inevitability of winter.

The idea of snow and ice excited Rita. There was a quickening in her step and an energy unleashed that she'd not known existed. Daily, she ran the dogs and watched each one with careful interest, trying as she did to remember the things Mark and her father had told her to look for.

"Some dogs are just along for the ride," August had said and Rita could see that this was true by watching the tuglines that connected the dogs to the gangline. She weeded out three dogs from the twenty-two simply because they refused to pull their own weight.

Others seemed prone to problems, sporting everything from simple injuries to the inability to keep up. They were hard workers but just not cut out for long distances. Rita had no choice but to eliminate them.

Rita spent much of her time in Mark's company, listening while he told her things that could well make a difference out on the trail. She remembered her father's caution to always carry dry kindling for long runs, as well as extra food and boots.

Days were long and arduous, usually starting by five in the morning and not ending until nine and sometimes ten at night. There was always the necessity of seeing to the dogs.

Feeding, grooming, doctoring, running—all of these activities took precedence over nearly everything else. Then there was the work with the race sleds, harnesses, and assorted items that Rita would need to take with her when she raced the Iditarod. The work seemed never ending and, as the student, Rita was frequently overwhelmed.

As autumn moved toward winter, Rita found herself actually enjoying the work and the company. It worried her, because often she found herself concentrating too much on what Mark was doing, whether it had anything to do with her training or not.

It was on one particular Saturday when Rita learned that Mark wouldn't be joining them, that she actually found herself asking her father why.

"Mark has to fill in for one of the patrolmen," August replied to his daughter's question. He had come to notice that Rita was far more accepting of Mark's participation in her training. Maybe Rita was changing.

"So then," Rita said with a smile, "it'll be just you and me today?"

"You, me, and your mother," August replied without a thought.

"But, Mom's not out here with us," Rita commented. Her mother had never been one to take a great deal of interest in the kennel.

"I'm sure she's got enough to keep her busy in the house," August said, untangling a long length of rope. "She always has run a tight ship. Even when she owned that roadhouse near Northway. Her boarders never lacked for anything. I can vouch for that."

"I'm sure that's true," Rita answered and sought to change the subject. "When do you think we'll get our first snow?"

"I'm not sure," August said, glancing up at the gray sky.

"It doesn't feel like it just yet, but soon. Probably in another couple of weeks."

"I can hardly wait," Rita said wistfully. She longed to run the dogs on snow again and get the feel of handling the team behind a basket.

"You're doing good work," August said, offering the praise Rita craved. "I just know you'll be more than ready when March gets here."

"Dad, do you think I should run any of the shorter races first?" Rita took the rope from her father and hung it on a nearby nail.

"Rules say you have to have written proof of at least one sanctioned race of two hundred miles or more," August replied.

"Which races should I participate in?" Rita asked.

"You could warm up with some of the shorter sprint races. As far as a race of some distance, Mark thinks the Copper Basin 300 is your best bet. It's run in January and it's close to home. The terrain will be similar to that which the dogs are already used to and yet offer them the feeling of competition and crowds," August answered thoughtfully.

Rita remained silent while considering her father's words.

"It would give you a good chance to get to know some of the other racers and dogs," August continued. "And you might even make a name for yourself before the Iditarod."

"That could be bad though," Rita replied. "It could put a lot of pressure on me to perform. Say I did really well in one race or another, then I'd be expected to achieve an even better performance in the Iditarod."

"That is a possibility," August said. "But, it could also be a challenge, and I know how competitive you can be."

"You sound like that's a fault and not an asset," Rita said with a frown. "There's nothing wrong with healthy competition."

"Healthy competition, no," August agreed. "However, competition can often lead to dangerous rivalry. Many mistakes are made by the person who thinks nothing of the rules and only of the achievement."

Rita shrugged off her father's concerns as she always had done in the past. It was impossible for him to understand her sense of competition. After all, he'd been an only son with a single sister to round out the family. He knew nothing of being the youngest of ten. When you were the baby of a huge family you always found yourself striving to make a place for yourself, Rita reasoned. Her father simply misunderstood her need.

"You know," August began, "I may sound a little old-fashioned, but I'd like for you to make your own sled."

Rita shook her head adamantly. "I wouldn't be any good at that. You know I've never had the touch for creating things that you have."

"But it's the only way to get a real feel for your equipment. Once you've been a part of creating the sled, it truly becomes a part of you. When it starts to run rough, you know instinctively what's wrong. When a piece breaks, you know from having created it, just what's required to repair it," August answered.

"I guess that makes sense," Rita admitted. "But I don't know anything about it. You'll have a great deal to teach me."

"You're a quick student," August said with a laugh. "I tell you what, Monday we'll get started with the details."

"August," Beth called from the back door. "Gerald's on the telephone. He wants to talk to you."

"I'm coming," August answered and turned to Rita. "You keep on sorting out these ropes and harnesses." Rita nodded and watched as her father headed toward the house.

She felt a twinge of disappointment in having to share her father with her oldest brother. She scarcely knew Gerald even though he settled in Tok. Gerald and Phillip were her mother's sons from her first marriage. Rita had heard many times, the story of how her mother and father met.

Her mother was a war widow, having lost her Canadian husband in World War II. Beth Hogan was running a roadhouse and trying to raise her children all alone when August had appeared to work on the Alcan Highway. Gerald and Phillip had appealed to August's heart, as had their mother, and, in no time at all, they became a family.

After that, many children came to bless the home of August and Beth Eriksson, but Rita saw it more as a curse. She hated being the youngest and felt completely insignificant to her family.

Plopping down on the ground, Rita tried to ignore the anger she felt. Many people presumed that because she was the baby of the family, she surely would have enjoyed the most attention. However, nothing could have been farther from the truth.

"I've scarcely seen you," Beth commented, causing Rita to jump.

"I've been busy," Rita offered, refusing to look her mother in the eye.

"Yes, your father has told me," Beth replied. "He also tells me that you still seem very unhappy."

Rita's dark eyes flashed a warning as her head snapped up to meet her mother's face. "I'm just busy," she stated firmly. "This is hard work, you know." Rita knew the words sounded sarcastic, but she didn't care.

"You needn't take that tone with me, Rita," Beth said, standing her ground. "I won't cower beneath your anger and you can't wile your way around the issues with me. That's why you avoid me."

"I don't avoid you," Rita answered, tossing the harness aside and getting to her feet. "I avoid your preaching. You can't have a regular conversation with me. You never just want to know how I am, or what I've been doing. You just want to pass judgment on me because I ruined your track record at church!"

Beth was noticeably hurt by the harsh words Rita hurled. "I'm sorry you feel that way, Rita. I do care about the things you're doing. I care very much."

"Yes, yes, I know. You care only because no matter what I do, it'll be wrong in your eyes," Rita said, trying to show nothing but the anger she felt inside. "I can't live up to your standards, Mother, so why not just give up?"

"I can't give up," Beth replied and pulled her sweater closer to ward off the cold. "It isn't my standards I want you to live up to. God's standards are the only ones that count."

"Yes, and you and God are like this," Rita said, and intertwined her first two fingers.

"Don't take that tone with me," Beth snapped. Her anger was piqued—a typical reaction whenever she spoke with her youngest daughter about God. Why, out of ten children, was this one the most difficult? "I cherish my relationship with God," Beth continued. "He is the only constant in our lives. He is the only one that can offer us hope and eternal salvation. I only want you to come to understand His love for you."

"I've heard it all before, Mom," Rita answered impatiently. "I don't need your religion. I grew up all my life listening to preaching—yours, the pastor's, even Dad's. I've had enough preaching to last me a lifetime. Why can't you understand that I don't need a crutch like you do? I make my own way, and when I know what I want. . .I go after it."

"And what do you want, Rita?" Beth asked her daughter honestly.

"I want to live my life without restraints. I want to experience everything and anything. I don't want to be hemmed in by a list of dos and don'ts. Besides," Rita continued, "I don't see where your relationship with God has helped you in your relationship with me."

Beth swallowed hard to keep from snapping a retort. It was true. She struggled to have a decent relationship with her youngest daughter. There was always so much hostility to get through that Beth usually gave up long before Rita wore down.

"You are absolutely right. Our relationship lacks for much," Beth answered softly. "But, I'm always hopeful. You may have grown up and left home, but I will continue to endeavor to help you see the truth, and God's love for you."

"It's always God's love, isn't it?" Rita questioned. "Never your love or our relationship. You use God like a shelter you can hide in whenever things get too tough. Learn to deal with me, one on one, Mom. I don't need this constant triangle. Then again," Rita said, turning to leave, "don't bother to deal with me at all."

Beth stood fixed to her spot as Rita walked off toward the creek. She was no longer shocked by her daughter's attitude and words. After all the years she'd sought to find a way to reach Rita, Beth had nearly given up trying. How could one child hold so much anger and hate inside and never give a clue as to where it came from or how it could be dealt with?

Walking slowly back to the house, Beth found herself whispering a prayer for Rita. It was really her only recourse,

Beth decided. Rita had made it quite clear that she didn't want to talk about it, so Beth would leave her to God.

"Where's Rita?" August asked as he met Beth at the door.

"We had words," Beth admitted. "She stormed off to the creek and I'm here licking my wounds."

August enfolded Beth in his arms. "Don't lose hope, Bethany," he encouraged. "God has had worse cases to deal with."

Beth smiled. "She takes after her father where stubbornness is concerned."

"Ah, so you do remember," August replied with a grin. It had been Beth's honest determination that had led him back to God so many years earlier. "I guess I was just about as tough a nut as God ever had to crack. I remember feeling so angry that I couldn't join the army and fight in World War II. I blamed God for my misfortune of having no wife and no children. Now, I have ten beautiful children and a gorgeous wife, but only after I came back to Him first. Rita will come to understand the truth one day. We just have to hold on to that."

"I know you're right, August. But it hurts so much. Why does she hate me the way she does?" Beth questioned in a trembling voice.

"I don't believe she hates you, sweet. I think she's just so miserable in herself and you are the closest reminder of what she could be if she turned her life over to God. I think that causes her more grief than she can own up to," August stated, giving Beth a squeeze. "You just keep praying, Mrs. Eriksson. Even the prodigal son in the Bible came home."

Beth tried to smile, but her heart was much too heavy. "Will you talk to her?" she questioned.

"For what it's worth," August said, dropping his hold on Beth. Beth nodded and watched for several minutes as

August made his way past the pile of harnesses and ropes that Rita had left in disarray. She whispered a prayer for her husband and then another one for her daughter. Surely God could work a miracle in the heart of her hurting child.

≈

"I thought I might find you here." August came upon Rita where she stood beside the icy creek. "I understand you and your mother had a fight."

"What else do we ever have? Certainly not a relationship." Rita's sarcasm hung thickly in the air.

August kicked at the dirt thoughtfully. "Your mother cares a great deal about you, Rita."

"Oh, I can certainly see that," Rita said sardonically, and turned her back to her father. No sense in letting him see the tears that had formed in her eyes.

"I felt just like you did when I was younger," August remembered. "When I met your mom, I was a hard man with a grudge against God. I felt like God had disappointed me one time too many and therefore I didn't want anything more to do with Him."

"I've heard this story before," Rita muttered.

"I know," the aging August answered. "But, it seemed important to share it with you one more time. Your mom confronted me with my hard heart and even though she loved me, she watched me walk away because she had the guts to stand up to me."

Rita said nothing. She stuffed her hands deep into her jeans' pockets to ward off the chill. If only there was someplace to warm her frozen heart.

"Well, anyway," August said, running a hand through his salt-and-pepper hair, "I kept thinking about the things she'd shared with me, and the way she assured me God was still there for me. I ran as far and as fast as I could and finally

God pinned me down in a place I couldn't fight Him anymore."

"I know," Rita replied. "He buried you under a construction tractor after you fell over the embankment." Rita remembered the story from its many tellings. Her father's tractor had plummeted over a soft shoulder as he graded roadway. He had been pinned beneath the equipment, broken and bleeding, and God had spoken to his spirit.

"I know it sounds silly," August admitted with a grin. "But sometimes God has to get your attention. He'd done everything else He could, but my stubbornness required drastic measures."

"Look, Dad," Rita began, turning to face her father. "Couldn't we just drop the subject? Isn't it enough that I know how you feel, and you know how I feel?"

"You mean agree to disagree?" August questioned.

"Yes." Rita came to her father and put both hands on his shoulders. "I love you, Dad, and I need for you not to harp at me. Mother has preaching down to a fine art form and I'd just as soon not have you hassling me as well."

"All right, Rita." August embraced his daughter. "I'll leave it be. At least for now."

"Thanks, Dad," Rita whispered. She couldn't help but wonder how she'd deal with her mother, but maybe if she put it off long enough she wouldn't have to do anything about it. Maybe Beth would just leave well enough alone and realize that Rita was a grown woman with a mind of her own.

five

The first snows fell and autumn quickly became winter. Rita was in better physical shape than she'd ever been, and her heart was eager for the challenge of the Iditarod.

After spending six months working with her dogs, Rita had chosen a team of fourteen, twice as many as the minimum requirement for the race. They were a hearty, well-bred group of dogs and Rita felt a genuine pride whenever she worked with them.

Week after week, Rita found herself engulfed in conversations that dealt with the business of dog sled racing, conversations that made her eager to feel the icy winds upon her face and the solitude of the long trail.

"You have to remember," Mark told Rita as she worked to attach the brush bow to the front of her handmade sled, "it's not always best to be out in front. If you head out early in the race and find the trail blown over, you may break trail through hip-high snow. . .maybe even higher. That's tedious, exhausting work, and the dogs pay a toll for it as well as the musher."

"So it's better to pace yourself behind?" Rita questioned. She sat up and adjusted the hood of her insulated sweatshirt.

"Sometimes, but not always. It's a matter of attitude and decision. You have to keep your mind cleared of other clutter and totally devoted to the trail. Then the choices are easier to make. You have to have a feel for the course. When you're out there all alone and faced with decisions like where to make your camp, and whether your dogs are up to another twenty miles without a rest, you realize that this is where experience, training, and attitude all make the difference between life and death."

"But how do you decide when it's right to take the risks when you've never run the Iditarod before?" Rita asked.

"Every Iditarod is different. No matter how many times you run it, you can't predict what the elements will be or how the terrain will have changed. Then, too, the route changes from year to year. From Anchorage to Ophir, it's the same trail for all years. After that however, the northern route, during the even years, goes up to Ruby from Ophir and down the Yukon River to Nulato and Kaltag, to name a few. The odd year, the southern route leaves Ophir and goes down to Iditarod and across to Anvik. From there you follow the Yukon up to Kaltag and then the race resumes identical trails again. And while I'm the first one to say that repeated experience on the trail is an important issue, it isn't everything."

Rita listened intently while Mark shared his secrets. She was still uncomfortable in his company, but she didn't feel the anger she once had. With so much else to concentrate on, Rita had less and less time to consider her lifelong struggle to find her niche.

"How's it going?" August asked as he joined Rita and Mark.

Rita gave her father a smile. "It's going slow," she replied honestly. "I told you this sled building thing wasn't my forte."

"But you've done very well," August encouraged. "Your first sled turned out great, and this lightweight racer will be even better. I think you're going to be pleased with the results."

"I think so, too," Mark agreed.

"I hope so," Rita said, thoughtfully checking her work for any errors.

"Are you two still planning on going out tomorrow?" August questioned, referring to the week-long sledding and camping trip that Rita and Mark had arranged.

"Yep," Mark answered before Rita could comment. "We're all set and the dogs are more than anxious. I figure we'll take out around dawn and be back in a week, maybe ten days."

"Just like we used to do when we were younger, eh, Rita?" August teased.

"Something like that," Rita replied. She was still uncertain about spending time away from her father and out on the desolate trail with Mark.

"Look, I'm going to finish up here and go home. I still have some gear to take care of and dog food to pack. I'll mush over in the morning, and you be ready to leave by sunrise," Mark said, getting to his feet. "I hate being kept waiting," he added in a joking voice.

"Don't worry about me." Rita glance upward. Her heart did a jump as she caught Mark's warm brown eyes. She tried to steady her nerves and sound more severe than she felt. "I told you I could take care of myself," she added.

Mark laughed and gave a little bow. "Then I shall await the pleasure of your company on the trail tomorrow, ma'am." With that he was gone, and Rita stared after him, shaking her head.

"He's a good man, Rita," August said as if reading the question on his daughter's mind. "I trust him, and I know he'll take good care of you on the trail. Trust him, Rita. He might very well teach you something you don't know."

Rita nodded slowly and gave her father a brief smile. Trust him? She didn't even know him outside the realm of the Eriksson dog kennel. Why should she believe him to be so trustworthy?

"Dad?" Rita questioned with a sudden thought. "I'd like to have a pistol. May I borrow one of yours?"

August nodded. "That's a good idea. I'll make sure you have one for the Iditarod, too. Sometimes it's necessary to put down an animal. You can never tell when a moose is going to jump in the middle of your dog team. It's happened before and they almost always have to be shot."

"I remember a moose wrecking havoc with one of the mushers several years back," Rita agreed.

"I do, too," August replied. "I'll make sure you have what you need."

"I have you, Daddy." Rita jumped up to hug her father. "And you are all I'll ever need."

August embraced his daughter but said nothing. He certainly couldn't tell her what was in his heart. He couldn't explain that she needed the Savior, and that without Him, she would be hopelessly lost. Breathing a silent prayer, August gave his youngest daughter over to God, knowing that there was really little else he could do.

&

The wind had picked up and the sky threatened snow, but nevertheless, Rita and Mark, with lamps secured on their heads, mushed out into the darkness with their dog teams. They had decided to explore the area to the south and maybe even check out the trail for the Copper Basin 300.

The snow wasn't all that deep, but it had glazed over with ice from a recent warming and refreezing. It made a good trail and Rita was surprised to learn that Mark had already spent many hours in the area, choosing the path they would take.

When they stopped for lunch, several hours later, Mark explained.

"I wanted this first day to be rather simple. You know, that way you could get used to the trail and being out away from civilization. And, it wouldn't be all that taxing for the dogs. We'll make camp about twelve miles down the way. There's a nice place by the river where we can set up camp under the trees. We'll have all the water we need and plenty of shelter," Mark told Rita.

"I didn't realize you had this all mapped out," Rita replied. She enjoyed some warmed-up tuna casserole her mother had sent along.

Mark stirred up the fire enjoying himself and the freedom of the vast wilderness before him. "I am the teacher, remember?" His words were spoken in a gentle reminder and for once Rita knew in order to object, she'd have to work hard to conjure up her anger.

"I just meant that I didn't realize you'd spent so much time and preparation on this trip. I figured we were just kind of heading out into the great unknown," Rita answered.

"After today," Mark replied, "we will be. I haven't planned every detail out. Rest assured there will be many elements of surprise on our adventure." He lost himself for a moment looking into Rita's eyes. She quickly captured his heart. Turning away before Rita could perceive his thoughts, Mark called over his shoulder, "You ready to press on?"

"More than ready," Rita responded, unaware of Mark's emotions.

They broke camp and pressed to the south. The valley floor soon gave way to foothills and dense forests of black and white spruce, as well as aspen and birch. From time to time, stunted black spruce and the absence of hardwood trees betrayed the sure signs of permafrost ground. This was ground that never thawed and nothing rooted well in it's frozen subsoil.

It reminded Rita of the parable of the sower. The seeds that fell upon the rocky soil couldn't take deep root. She shook off the image wondering why she'd even thought of it. No doubt eighteen years of Bible stories and Sunday school had to exist in memory somewhere. Sending the reminder of her mother and father's faith deeper within the dark recesses of her memories, Rita pressed on to keep pace with Mark.

Without warning, a snowshoe hare darted out across the trail causing Rita's team to take off in a free-for-all chase. Rita struggled to keep her grip on the sled's handlebars. She wouldn't forgive herself if she lost her team, especially in front of Mark.

"Gee, Dandy!" she yelled above the barking huskies, trying to tell her dogs to go back around to the right. By now, they were nearly heading in the opposite direction from which Rita and Mark had been making their way. "Come gee! Dandy, come gee!" Rita called out. When Dandy finally heard his mistress's instructions, he managed to direct the team back to the trail, much to the disappointment of the other ten dogs behind him.

Rita tried not to look flustered, but she was keenly aware that Mark watched and evaluated her every move from where he'd brought his own dogs to a stop back on the trail. Expecting some sarcastic comment regarding the incident,

Rita was surprised when Mark turned back around and called out the command that sent his dogs forward. Breathing a sigh of relief, Rita tried to be more prepared for any more interferences with her team.

❧

Shortly before the last bits of muted sunlight faded from the sky, Mark brought them, without further mishap, to the place he'd planned for their first night on the trail.

Rita put up her small domed tent only after seeing to the needs of her dogs. August had explained to her on many occasions that the dogs were her life's blood on the trail. Taking care of them first insured that they'd be in prime condition to take care of her later.

Rita found spruce boughs and made beds for each of her dogs, while a roaring fire heated up August's personal choice of dog food. It was a hearty combination of commercial dog food blended with beef liver, vegetable oil, and eggs. All were chosen to give the highest degree of benefit to the active sled dog.

With the dogs now fed and sleeping in fuzzy balls to ward off the minus twenty degree winds, Rita found herself able to settle down to preparing her own supper.

"I've already got the stew on the fire," Mark offered when he spied Rita digging into the food packs.

"I'm glad," Rita replied, plopping down beside the fire. "I'm absolutely starved." It felt good to sit and rest, even in frosty air that stung her eyes.

"I'd kind of like some coffee," Mark said, pulling out a zippered bag of instant coffee.

"That does sound good," Rita agreed. While Mark found cups, Rita studied the surroundings. She realized how perfect their camp was. They were sheltered from the wind by a rocky ridge that followed the river for a short ways. This was coupled with the canopy of spruce trees that lined the river.

They also had water—even if they did have to break the surface ice with an ax. With a little more effort, they soon had enough firewood to enjoy the evening, allowing both of them to sit back and bask in the warmth. Mark had been very wise to choose this place, Rita decided. A part of her wanted to tell him so; another part warned her not to make any kind of comment that betrayed her emotions.

Supper passed in relative silence. Mark seemed content to enjoy the quiet and the meal, while Rita nervously wondered how to relate to her traveling companion. Always before their talk had revolved around sledding, dogs, and the Iditarod. What if she were required to talk of something more?

As if reading her mind, Mark began to speak. "You know it's hard to sit out here in the middle of nowhere, with all of this monumental beauty around you and not be in awe of it."

"It is impressive," Rita agreed in a guarded tone. "It makes it hard to consider leaving."

"Leaving?" Mark questioned. "Where would you go?"

Rita shrugged. "I don't know. I've thought about moving to Texas."

Mark chuckled. "Cowboys and oil wells instead of dog sleds and snow?"

"I don't know. It was just a thought," Rita replied. "I've always liked the things I've read about it. Lots of sunshine and wide open spaces. You can have it rustic and rural or live it up in the glamourous city night life. I guess Texas has a little bit of everything."

"Maybe I could call you Texas Rita," Mark joked, but

Rita just lifted her chin defiantly.

"Maybe you wouldn't need to call me anything."

Mark hid his smile and turned away from Rita. There was no sense in irritating her further. "Look," Mark said and pointed to a glowing green light that loomed up from the horizon and grew in size until it seemed to fill the sky.

Rita watched as it changed in shape and size. The green soon gave way to a more prominent outline of pink and then, as the color intensified and darkened to a reddish hue, yellow fiery flickers sent fingers upward through the image to paint the sky.

"The northern lights," Rita commented as she watched the night show. "I've always loved them."

"I just don't know how anyone could watch them and doubt the existence of God," Mark said in a low husky whisper.

"What's God have to do with it?" Rita said rather flippantly. "It's a natural phenomenon. I read all about it and it has something to do with the sun."

Mark turned from the light show to study Rita a moment before replying. "I don't understand how you could have spent years in church and fellowship with other Christians and say such a shallow thing."

Rita instantly felt defensive. Obviously, Mark was yet another devout Christian. Why hadn't she considered that before? There wouldn't have been any way at all that her father would have taken on a less than fully devoted man of God, as his partner. Oh, she knew her father had told her Mark was a good man and a Christian, but since Mark had never bothered to make it an issue with her, Rita had felt safe to let things lie undisturbed.

"Look," Rita said with only the slightest hint of irritation in her voice, "I've tried to look at things like my folks, and apparently you do. I've joined all the groups, read all the Bible handouts, prayed all the prayers, and held my head just so when the minister preached his sermons. I've spent a lifetime being preached at, prayed at, and talked at and, as shallow as it might seem to you, I just don't feel the same way you do."

"I think that's the most honesty you've given me since we met," Mark remarked in a way Rita hadn't expected. It so flabbergasted Rita that she said nothing as Mark continued. "I know how hard it is to feel like God is real. I went through a bad time of that myself. People kept saying, 'Well if you just believed the way you should, you'd understand.' Then they'd all kind of stand around with this knowing look, all nodding at each other like I'd missed the joke. I hated it."

"Exactly," Rita said, totally amazed that Mark actually had put her feelings into words. "Or they give you that little shake of their head, where you can practically hear the 'Tisk, tisk' under their breath and they talk about turning you over to God to be dealt with. Like you were a sack of potatoes that needed to be washed up for dinner."

Mark chuckled out loud, momentarily breaking the tension. "My favorite one was when they'd tell me that my faith wasn't strong enough. 'Just have faith,' they'd say. Faith is the key. Faith is the answer. Faith is your foundation. And then they'd never tell me how it was I was suppose to get it, keep it, or understand it."

"I can't believe we're having this conversation," Rita said suddenly. "My parents would never understand. Especially my mother."

"You and your mom have a difficult relationship, don't

you?" Mark spoke the words hesitantly. He worried that if he prodded Rita to reveal too much, too soon, she'd bolt and run like a frightened deer.

"That's the understatement of the century. Negotiating peace among warring nations would be a simpler project than dealing with our relationship," Rita retorted.

"I would imagine that makes it quite difficult for you." Mark's words pulled Rita out of her defensive mode for once in her life.

"That's really the first time any one has ever mentioned that our relationship might be hard on me. Usually, there's all this sympathy for my mother," Rita stated with a sadness to her voice. "She has a prayer group. . .you know the type. It's made up of the local church women and they all pray for the issues of the day. My mother never hesitates to tell me that they've been praying for me for roughly the last twenty-some years. It's no wonder that people see things her way. She probably goes to the meetings and pours out her heart and cries her miseries of life with a difficult child. It drove me from home and now that I'm back, nothing has changed."

"And exactly what is it that hasn't changed?" Mark asked, throwing another log on the fire.

Rita grew quiet for a moment, and Mark thought for certain he'd pushed her too far. When she finally spoke, he realized he'd been holding his breath and exhaled it rather loudly.

"My mother can't deal with me as a daughter. I'm nothing more to her than a challenge. A soul to win to God so that her tally sheet is complete when she stands before her King. She's never cared for me as a mother would a child, and I resent the only concern she bears for me is that which is on the behalf of another."

"And this is also why you resist a relationship with God?" Mark asked without thinking.

"I picked up the Bible as a young girl," Rita said, turning. Mark's expression was gentle. "I was thinking about giving my life over to Him. I really was. But I opened the Bible to Isaiah and a verse that put me off in a way that even now causes me grief."

"What was it?"

"It said something like, 'As a mother comforts her child, so God comforts His people.' I'd never known anything but pain and frustration from my mother. Certainly not comfort and if God was as comforting as my mother, then that meant nothing to me. I slammed the Bible shut and sulked for weeks. I had never felt more betrayed." Rita got to her feet and walked a few steps from the fire before turning around briefly. Her eyes narrowed slightly, blinking back tears. "I'm sorry. I should never have told you these things."

Mark watched Rita walk to the river's edge. She just stood there for several minutes, looking out as if seeking peace for her soul. He allowed her the time to compose herself before he joined her.

"I'm glad you talked to me," he whispered at her back. "I think it helps friends to understand one another when they know each other's pain."

"Friends?" Rita questioned, whirling around to find herself only inches from Mark. "I thought you didn't want to be my friend."

Mark smiled through the shadowy light. Rita noted the change in his eyes. "I'd like to be much more," Mark said before pulling Rita into his arms and kissing her.

Rita was shocked into silence and passive acceptance. She

found herself enjoying the kiss, while she fought in her mind to resist the pleasure of Mark's touch. Warnings went off in her brain. Don't get too close! Don't care too much! Don't reciprocate!

When Mark released her, Rita shook her head and took a step backward. Mark reached out to steady her as she found her foot give way on the unstable river bank.

"Let me go," she whispered without malice. She sidestepped Mark and felt his grip give way when her feet were fixed on firm ground. Without looking behind her, Rita hurried breathlessly to her tent and the solitude it afforded her.

six

Rita returned from her sled trip more withdrawn and quiet than before. She purposefully went out of her way to avoid Mark and very little was offered in the way of explanation.

August and Beth watched on helplessly. How were they to help this child who so obviously didn't want their help? They sat alone in their kitchen one evening, long after Rita had retired for the night. Holding each other's hands as they shared a prayer, August and Beth found comfort in the Lord and each other.

"I'm really afraid for her," Beth said after August ended the prayer. "She's so miserable and unhappy with her life. She wants to blame everyone else for her problems. Do you know that she told me she would never have bothered to come home except for the fact that her college roommate had decided to move to the Lower Forty-eight. Never mind the Iditarod. It was as if she couldn't accept that she'd made the choice to come home all by herself."

"I'd hoped things would be different," August admitted, pouring himself another cup of coffee. When he offered to pour Beth a cup, she shook her head.

"Did Mark say anything about their trip?" Beth questioned, curiously.

"He mentioned that he kissed her," August said with a half smile. "But she made it clear that he was to keep his distance and, well, you know Mark. He's a good man and he put it behind him."

"Does she still plan to race?" Beth asked.

"As far as I know," August answered with a shrug of his

shoulders. "But with Rita, who can ever be sure. It wouldn't surprise me at all if she came downstairs tomorrow with her bags in hand." Beth nodded and said nothing. What else could be said?

❧

Rita didn't show up the following morning with bags in hand, nor was her disposition as sour as it had been upon her return. She had just answered her mother's inquiry about what she'd like for breakfast when a knock sounded at the front door.

"I wonder who that is?" August put down his newspaper.

"I'll get it, Dad," Rita offered and took off for the front room.

"Aunt Julie!" August heard his daughter squeal in excitement.

"Julie?" August said and exchanged a look of surprise with Beth. "Julie said nothing about visiting." He got to his feet and met his sister and daughter halfway.

"Jewels," he said, using her nickname, "why didn't you tell us you were coming?"

"Sam and I wanted to surprise you," the white-haired Julie replied. She hugged August through her bulky knee-length coat.

"Where is your husband?" August questioned. He and Sam had been best friends long before Sam had married Julie. It must have been a lifetime ago when they'd all lived in Nome. "It's been years since I've seen him."

"You know Sam," Julie answered. "He's out there getting our things."

"I'll give him a hand," Rita said, but Julie waved her off.

"Don't bother," Julie replied. "There's already a nice young man out there helping him."

"That would be Mark," August offered. "He's the partner

I wrote you about."

"Seems like a great guy," Julie said as Beth came into the room. "Bethany, you look great. Eastern Alaska must not take the toll on a body that western Alaska does. You look a hundred years younger than I feel."

Beth laughed and reached out to embrace Julie. "It's just the traveling that makes you feel that way. I know you. After a good rest, you'll be down here teaching me some new recipe or sewing shortcut."

"I told her this was a vacation," Sam called from the doorway. "She'd better take it easy. After all, that is what the doctor told her to do."

"Are you sick, Jewels?" August asked in a serious tone.

"I had pneumonia," Julie admitted. "But I'm much better now."

"Well, you will take it easy while you're here," Beth said, ushering Julie down the hall. "I have the perfect room for you. Remember the way the girls used to have the greenhouse bedroom all fixed up? Well, I have taken the project back on."

The group followed Beth to the bedroom. On one wall were huge double doors that Beth opened to reveal a greenhouse filled with potted plants.

"It's beautiful!" Julie exclaimed. "Imagine all that green in the dead of winter."

"It's well insulated, too," August said, moving aside for Mark to bring in the luggage he'd wrangled away from Sam.

"By the way," Mark said and placed the bags on the highly polished, wooden floor, "I'm Mark Williams."

Sam took his hand and shook it vigorously. "You know who I am already, but this here is my wife, Julie. She's August's sister."

"Yes, I know," Mark replied as he took Julie's hand and

held it. "August has spoken most fondly of you."

Julie exchanged a look of love with her brother. They had always been close and even when August had moved so far from Nome, he'd managed to keep Julie and Sam as important parts of his life.

Rita took the opportunity to slip from the room. She hated herself for leaving without getting an opportunity to talk with her aunt, but there would be time for that later.

She quickly made her way to the back porch where she retrieved her insulated coveralls and boots. She had finished dressing to tend the dogs, when Mark appeared.

"Are you going to keep avoiding me?" he asked in a gentle voice.

Rita made the mistake of meeting his eyes. "I, uh. . .," her words trailed into silence. She wanted to say more, but the words were stuck in her throat.

"Well?" he pushed.

"I don't want to talk about it," Rita stated firmly and started past him.

"Rita," Mark called and took hold of her arm.

"I don't want to talk to you right now," Rita repeated. "Don't you understand? You are annoying me with this pressure."

"What are you afraid of?" Mark asked her. He dropped his hand and waited for her reply.

Rita's eyes flashed the warning that her anger had been piqued. "I'm not afraid of anything, and I don't owe you any explanations. You've trained me now, and I can make the Iditarod a reality without any more interference from you."

"Where is all this fury coming from?" Mark asked. "Is this because I kissed you or because you opened up to me?"

Hitting the raw nerves that made up Rita's emotions, she quickly lowered her head to avoid Mark's reading her eyes.

She knew that saying nothing was like surrendering, but in truth, she was afraid to say anything. Pushing past him, Rita made her way to the dogs.

Mark stood on the steps watching her walk away. When had he come to care so much about this hurting woman-child? He was almost afraid to search himself for the depth of his concern. What if he learned more than he was willing to deal with?

❧

Rita's opportunity to speak in private with her Aunt Julie presented itself the following morning. Beth and August had volunteered to take Sam and Julie shopping in Tok, and when Julie chose instead to stay home, Rita offered to keep her company.

Preparing them both some hot tea, Rita took two steaming mugs with her to Julie's greenhouse sitting room.

"I'm so glad you came here," Rita stated bluntly, handing Julie the tea. "I've always been able to talk to you, even when I couldn't talk to Mom or Dad. You never seemed to judge me or make me feel inadequate."

"I knew you needed me," Julie replied. "I felt the most overwhelming need to keep you in my prayers and not for the reasons you think, so stop frowning. I'm not going to start preaching at you, I just knew you needed some extra care."

"Thanks," Rita managed, a bit uncomfortably.

"Now, why don't you tell me what's bothering you?" Julie smiled.

For the next two hours, Rita shared her heart with her aunt. She mentioned her mother's attitude and her worries about her father's advanced years to which Julie only laughed.

"We aren't that many years apart you know," Julie remarked. "And I feel fit as a fiddle. Of course, Sam and I know we aren't young kids anymore. In fact, it wouldn't surprise me at all if one of us were to die in the near future."

Rita frowned at her aunt's words. "I don't like to think about that. I don't know how you can talk so unemotionally about it, either."

"Rita, you don't like to talk about it because you're young and because you don't know what the future holds for you after death. That's all. Sam and I aren't afraid to die. Oh, we don't like the idea of the separation here on earth, but we know that it won't be for long, and then we can share eternity in Heaven."

"You make it sound so wonderful," Rita replied with a weak smile. "I know that Dad feels the same way. I guess it's just my selfishness that keeps me worried."

"Rita, I think it's fear, not selfishness that keeps you bothered. For all of your life, I've never seen you a single time without the fear in your eyes. What is it that you're so afraid of?"

The words rang in her ears. Mark had asked her the same questioned. What was she afraid of?

"I don't know," Rita answered with a heavy sigh. "I try not to believe that I'm afraid of anything. It makes you vulnerable to be afraid."

"And vulnerability is probably what you fear the most," Julie replied. "Vulnerability means that you aren't one-hundred percent in control. Vulnerability means that someone might see something more than the façade of independence you wear. Vulnerability might mean that someone will get too close to you."

"Yes," Rita admitted.

"Why do you fear getting close to others?" Julie asked softly.

Rita put her cup down and paced the room. "I don't know. I guess because it hurts so much when they reject you."

"And who rejected you, Rita?" Julie pressed on.

"Lots of people," Rita answered. "My brothers and sisters never had much to do with me. Even my own mother. . . ." her thoughts fell short of words. "I don't really want to talk about them. I'm having a problem, however, with Mark Williams."

"He seems nice enough," Julie replied.

"He is," Rita said and stopped. "That's the problem. I've managed to put off every guy who's ever shown the slightest bit of interest in me. I knew I wanted to go to college and become a nurse like you, and I knew that someday I wanted to race in the Iditarod. A man would interfere with that."

"I once worried about the same thing," Julie laughed. "It's so like God to put you through something so that you can be a help to someone else later down the road."

"What are you talking about?" Rita questioned.

"When I married Sam, I did so without ever really understanding how he felt about my career as a nurse. Remember, my job was with the Public Health Department and I was often dog sledding out to the villages for many weeks at a time. I didn't know how to talk about my fears to Sam. I just knew that he would never approve."

"But he did, didn't he?"

"Yes, he did," Julie remembered. "He had it all planned out ahead of time to be with me on the trail. So for the most part, Sam joined me whenever I had to be gone for long periods of time. Eventually, I learned we were to have a baby and so I quit my job and planned to stay home for a spell. Of course, you know that our son died when he was very small."

Rita nodded. "Why didn't you have other children?"

"I wanted to. I learned that I was to have another baby only three months after little Sam's death. But, I miscarried and nearly bled to death. They had to perform a hysterectomy and that meant no more children."

"I'm sorry, Aunt Julie," Rita said sadly. "I never knew."

"It's all right, Rita. God had other plans for Sam and me. We learned a great deal just being together, and we worked well as a team among the Eskimos and Indians. I have no regrets and have thoroughly enjoyed my life. But in order to do so, I became very vulnerable."

"I can well imagine," Rita said in a barely audible voice. "I'm just not sure that I could deal with it as well."

"A body never knows what it can endure until it goes through it. You're planning on putting yourself to a detailed test of the elements, wills, and survival when you race from Anchorage to Nome. You will be vulnerable because of the position you place yourself in. Do you want to back away from the responsibility of the Iditarod, just because of that challenge?" Julie asked her niece.

"Well, no," Rita shook her head.

"You like this Mark, don't you?" Julie questioned again. "That's why this situation has become so disturbing to you. It's why your mother's words about God are so frightening to you. You know the truth about God. How could you not? You were raised in an atmosphere of Christian love. You attended church on your first outing after birth. Yet, even with all of this knowledge and wisdom at your fingertips, you chose instead to turn away from God's love. Why is that, Rita?"

"I don't know," Rita answered, forgetting to be angry that Julie had referenced salvation.

"I think you do," Julie replied. "You don't trust yourself

enough to love God or Mark."

"What?" Rita questioned as her head snapped up to meet her aunt's eyes. "What in the world has trusting myself got to do with loving God or Mark?"

Julie shifted uncomfortably in the wicker chair. Rita jumped up to retrieve a pillow while she waited for her aunt's insight.

"Thank you, dear," Julie said as she eased against the cushioning bulk. "Now, what I was trying to help you see is the huge mistrust you have in yourself. I think you're the only one who can say why it's there, but its effects are clear. God stands with open arms, offering a free gift of love and salvation. Mark apparently offers at least friendship, possibly more. In both cases, I don't believe it's God or Mark who frightens you the most. It's Rita. For whatever reason you have contrived, you don't believe yourself trustworthy and deserving of love."

Rita frowned and bit at her lower lip. Was her Aunt Julie right? Was this the demon from which she had so long run? Sitting back down, Rita seemed to withdraw into her thoughts to find the answers.

Julie reached out and covered Rita's hand with her own. "I know this is hard for you, but may I suggest something?"

Rita nodded.

"Good. I want to outline some Scripture for you. Maybe you can better understand what I'm saying and what God's plan is, if you read His Word. Now, don't get defensive with me, just trust me. I want you to read the verses I mark and just think about them. Then, if you want to talk to me about them, I'll be happy to share whatever I know. Deal?"

Rita hesitated for a moment. She looked into Julie's dark eyes. Eyes that held so much love and concern for Rita that she wanted to cry for the very need of it.

"All right, Aunt Julie," she finally answered. "It's a deal."

"And Rita," Julie added with a smile, "try not to be so hard on that young man. I think your father is an excellent judge of character, after all, he led me to my Sam. Mark may very well be a special gift for you. Maybe he'll only be a friend, maybe more. But you'll never know if you aren't decent to him. Just open your heart a bit. You might be surprised at the results."

Rita nodded slowly. "I'll try. But, it's those results that I'm worried about."

seven

Rita sat in the quiet solitude of her room. For the first time since she'd stopped going to church, she found a Bible spread out before her. Her Aunt Julie had given her several Scriptures to look up and most of them were in the first book of Corinthians.

Rita knew the Bible forward and backward, and as she turned to the thirteenth chapter of Corinthians, she already knew what the verses would say.

"Though I speak with the tongues of men and of angels, and have not charity, I am become as sounding brass, or a tinkling cynbal," the first verse began. Rita scanned the verses, remembering them well. She once had to quote the verses from memory in order to win a new Bible. It hadn't meant that much to her, but it seemed terribly important to her mother and father.

Then Rita quoted the fourth, fifth, and sixth verses aloud. "'Charity suffereth long, and is kind; charity envieth not; charity vaunteth not itself, is not puffed up, doth not behave itself unseemly, seeketh not her own, is not easily provoked, thinketh no evil; rejoiceth not in iniquity, but rejoiceth in the truth.'"

Rita stopped and thought immediately of her mother. *Love keeps no record of wrongs*, she thought. So much had passed between them. So many angry words, so much ugliness and hurt. If love truly kept no record of wrong, then maybe Rita didn't love her mother.

It was as though she'd had the wind knocked out of her.

Rita had realized the anger and distance she felt toward her mother, but never once had she considered that she might not love her.

Glancing down at the Bible, Rita read on about how love does not delight in evil but rejoices with the truth and that it always protects, always trusts, always hopes, always perseveres. She didn't feel that way at all toward her mother. She didn't trust her mother or understand her. How could she love her?

The realization bothered Rita more than she could bear. Where had they gone wrong? From where had the pain come? Rita stretched out across her bed and closed her eyes. In her mind she saw herself as a child, long black pigtails trailed down her back. Her mother had always insisted that Rita wear her hair long and Rita, in turn, hated it. But why?

Rita saw herself playing alone in her room. There were no other siblings her own age and nobody seemed to notice that she was lonely.

"Go play, Rita," she could hear her mother saying. She was fitting one of Rita's older sisters for her wedding dress.

"There's nobody to play with," answered a five-year-old Rita.

"Then just find something to do, Rita. I'm busy!" her mother had exclaimed in complete frustration.

Rita had walked away from the room, head hanging down like one of the dogs after being told "no" to some forbidden activity. She had almost made it to her room before hearing her mother tell her sibling how hard it was to live with Rita. There were other words, too. It was more pain than Rita wanted to deal with. Opening her eyes she thought instead of Mark Williams.

She couldn't deny that she enjoyed his kiss. Nor could

she ignore the way her heart had jumped at his touch. She saw his face in her mind and the soft, gentleness of his eyes. Rita buried her face in her pillow. Why were these things happening just when she should be clearheaded and single-minded. The race was in such a short time, and Rita knew she needed to devote her thoughts to it.

"If I hadn't read the Bible," Rita thought aloud, "this wouldn't be happening. This is why I don't like all this soul searching. It brings up things I'd rather not think of."

Rita thought of her Aunt Julie's words about trust. Rita didn't trust people and she didn't trust herself. Trusting meant opening yourself up to more hurt. It meant being vulnerable, and Rita believed when a person was vulnerable, others took advantage of you.

Rita was just starting to doze off when a knock sounded at the door. Getting wearily to her feet, Rita opened the door to find her father.

"Am I interrupting anything?" August asked.

"No, come on in, Dad. I was just about to go to bed." Rita stepped back.

August walked into the room and pulled Rita's desk chair up beside her bed. He noticed the Bible and although he wanted ask about it, August decided to let Rita bring it up.

"It's kind of early for you to be going to bed, isn't it?" August questioned. "You aren't sick are you?"

"No, Daddy," Rita said with a smile. "I'm just tired. It's been an exhausting day with the dogs, and then, of course, I've been doing a great deal of thinking about the race, and all the complications and problems we still have to overcome."

"There is a lot to consider," August agreed. "We need to finish buying your supplies for one thing. Then we have to arrange for transporting dog food and whatever else you'll need to the various checkpoints on the trail. I thought I'd send you and Mark over to Fairbanks tomorrow."

"Fairbanks? But that'll take a whole day coming and going," Rita protested. "Can't we get everything we need, in Tok?" What she really wanted to say was that she couldn't imagine having to bear Mark's company for a whole day without revealing her feelings. Then again, what were her feelings?

"We'll get some of the stuff in Tok, but there are several things I want you to pick up in Fairbanks," August replied.

"I could go alone," Rita offered.

"No," August answered. "Mark has things to pick up, as well. You'll need his help, and I know he'll enjoy your company."

"Why do you say that?" Rita asked, suddenly interested in what Mark might have said to her father.

August grinned. "It isn't hard to see that he cares for you."

"Has he said that?"

"Well, I suppose it wouldn't be fair to share our conversations with you. But, suffice it to say, his opinion of you is quite high." August reached out to take Rita's hand. "I get the feeling you're kind of fond of him as well."

Rita couldn't contain her surprise. "I don't know what you're talking about."

"Rita, this is me you're talking to," August said softly. "I've seen the way you watch Mark, and I've seen the way he watches you. I know there's a chemistry there, but I also know there are a lot of problems to overcome. Please believe me, I'm not trying to push a romance between you two. I just realize that you share an interest. Mark's a good man, Rita. You could do a lot worse."

"I know," Rita said, finally giving in. "He is nice, and I do enjoy his company. I'm just not ready for any relationships.

I hope you understand. I mean, I know you worry about me being alone, but don't. I'll be fine, Daddy."

"I don't think you're as tough as you'd like any of us to believe, Rita. But, nonetheless, I'll bide my time," August stated. "Now, are you up to the trip tomorrow?"

"Sure, but I really need to be careful. I'm running out of money fast," Rita answered.

"I've sold a couple of dogs," August said. "We have to have enough set aside to ship the supplies to the check-points, as well as the one thousand two hundred forty-nine dollars that it takes to register in the Iditarod. Your mother is making your dog booties and some of your insulated gear."

"She is?" Rita questioned in amazement.

"That's right. She's also freezing snacks for your dogs. She's making honeyballs right now," August said, refer-ring to a popular treat that many mushers used. The treats were made of lean beef, honey, powdered eggs, brewer's yeast, and vegetable oil. To this, vitamins and bonemeal were added and rolled into pieces the size of baseballs. It gave the dogs a tasty, high-protein snack that helped to meet the 10,000 calories a day that each dog needed to sustain energy on the trail.

Rita said nothing. She'd had no idea her mother was in-volved in making her Iditarod dream come true. It made Rita uncomfortable. Somehow it made her feel vulnerable.

"Now, have you kept track of the mandatory require-ments?" August continued. "You know about the maxi-mum ratings on the sleeping bag and the minimum weight requirements?"

"Sure, Daddy," Rita said, and recited the requirements for both. "I also need an ax with a head weighing at least one and three-quarters pounds, and the handle has to be at least twenty-two inches long. Then I need a pair of snow shoes thirty-three inches by eight inches, eight booties for each dog, one cooker, one pot capable of holding three gallons of water, two pounds of food for each dog, and one day's rations for myself. Oh, and it all has to fit on the sled. Did I leave out anything?"

August laughed. "Not as far as the mandatories go. You've done your homework, and I'm very proud of you. When you and Mark get back from Fairbanks, we'll start going over the critical points of the route itself." August got to his feet and studied his youngest daughter for a moment. She was willowy and graceful, but there was still a hardness to her that he didn't understand. "I love you, Rita," he said, turning to leave.

"I love you, too, Daddy," Rita called out. She noted the look of concern on her father's face and hoped silently that he wasn't feeling ill. She couldn't help but notice the way he seemed to slow down more and more each day.

Long after their conversation, Rita still lay awake in bed thinking of her father's interminable aging. She wished she could have known him as a young man, wished he could have parented her as a young man. In thought interwoven with images of Mark Williams, Rita finally fell into a restless sleep. Tomorrow she would spend a great deal of time alone with Mark, and the thought weighed as heavy on her mind as that of her father's strength and health.

～

For most of the trip into Fairbanks, Rita allowed Mark to set the conversation. She answered only when the situation required her to do so and refrained from offering her opinion when it did not. She stared out the window watching the endless spruce forest, now heavy with snow. The trees seemed to weave an impenetrable labyrinth across the landscape and Rita wished silently that she could lose herself out amongst them, rather than travel in confinement with Mark.

Mark sensed Rita's reluctance to open up to him, even before they'd climbed into his truck for the long trip. He wondered if her silence was due to her efforts to concentrate on the upcoming race, or something more personal.

Their business in Fairbanks passed swiftly and satisfactorily, and Rita was grateful that Mark had to see to many of his own needs. Before Rita slipped away to take care of a personal matter for her father, they agreed to meet back at the truck by three o'clock.

The jeweler's shop for which August had written the address for was only a block away from where Rita had parted company with Mark. She walked into the building, jingling the bells on the front door as she did. A gray-haired man in a dark blue business suit met her before she reached the counter.

"May I help you?" he asked in a rich baritone voice.

"I'm here to see Mr. Simons," Rita related. "My father sent me with this package and instructions that I am to pick up a gift he ordered for my mother."

"You must be Rita Eriksson," the man replied. "I'm Jim Simons." He extended a friendly hand forward that Rita took with less enthusiasm.

"I'm glad to meet you. This is the package my father sent me with," Rita stated, quickly dropping the man's hand. She handed the heavy box to Mr. Simons, halfway expecting him to open it. When he didn't, Rita couldn't contain her surprise. "If you need to look it over," she said, "I have time to wait."

"That isn't necessary at all," Mr. Simons replied. "Your father and I have already arranged the matter. I have your mother's gift already wrapped." Mr. Simons moved to the back side of the counter where he placed the package Rita had brought and retrieved a smaller, gift-wrapped box. "He'll find everything in order."

Rita nodded and took the gift.

"May I show you anything?" the man questioned. "I have some lovely necklaces just in and also there's a sale on some of my finest rings."

"I don't think so, thank you," Rita said with a glance at her watch. "I have to meet Mark, I mean my ride, at three o'clock and I still have a few more stops to make."

"Would your companion be Mark Williams?" Mr. Simons asked, surprising Rita.

"Why, yes," Rita answered. "How did you know?"

Mr. Simons laughed. "I guess that does seem a bit strange, doesn't it. I seemed to recall your father mentioning that you and Mr. Williams would be riding into town together. I have the wedding ring Mr. Williams picked out when he was here last weekend, and I presumed he would stop by today and pick it up. I wasn't certain, however, that it would be ready so I didn't call him ahead of time. If you would be so kind as to tell him that it's finished, I would sincerely appreciate it."

Rita felt as though she'd been delivered a blow. A wedding ring! Mark had never mentioned having a girl friend, much less someone he planned to marry. Trying hard to keep her astonishment to herself, Rita agreed to pass Mr. Simons's message on to his client.

Walking from the store, Rita tried not to let the news bother her. Of course Mark was free to see whomever he chose and marry whenever he decided to, but Rita was amazed that her father hadn't even alluded to fact that Mark was dating someone. In fact, Rita thought, her father had pushed her toward a relationship with Mark. Maybe he didn't know that Mark planned to marry someone else.

Unless. . . . Surely Mark hadn't bought the ring for Rita! No, Mark wouldn't do things that way. He was too straight-forward and honest. Honest to a fault, she thought.

Rita hadn't realized the apprehension and disappointment that was creeping into her heart. Had she really become more interested in her father's rugged business partner than she'd allowed herself to see?

"He's getting married," Rita muttered under her breath. "I would never have guessed it in a million years."

She made her other stops, barely able to concentrate on what she was doing, and made her way back to where Mark sat waiting in the pickup.

"Well, Texas Rita, get everything you were after?" he asked with a good-natured smile.

"I guess so," she answered, not even acknowledging the nickname. Rita looked up at him as if really seeing him for the first time. She felt saddened to realize they would never be more than friends. How could she have been so blind to the fact that she was falling in love with Mark Williams?

"Well then, we'd best head home. We can stop and pick up something to eat on the way out of town. That is, if you don't mind fast food," Mark said, reaching down to start the truck.

"I don't mind," Rita replied. She suddenly remembered Mr. Simons's request and reached out to prevent Mark from starting the engine. "I almost forgot. I had to pick up some-thing for Dad at Simons's Jewelry Store. Mr. Simons said to tell you that your package is ready."

Rita watched purposefully to catch Mark's reaction. He smiled broadly and patted his coat pocket. "I've already taken care of it," he answered.

Rita thought he seemed quite pleased with himself. She fastened her seat belt and nodded. "Then I'm ready to go," she said and turned to stare out the passenger window.

Aside from giving Mark her order for a hamburger, french fries, and iced tea, Rita was silent in her brooding.

"How could I have been so stupid as to let my guard down and get interested him?" she whispered to herself. She sighed and accepted the food that Mark had generously paid for.

Wasn't this exactly why she didn't allow herself to be vulnerable? The pain she was feeling brought it all back to her. She had to build the wall up higher to protect herself from ever feeling this way again. How could she have been so stupid?

Of course, she reasoned with herself, I never gave Mark the slightest bit of encouragement. He had no reason to believe I was interested. Rita made a pact with her heart that from that moment forward, she would care about nothing else but the Iditarod. She wouldn't allow herself to care about anyone else in a way that would distract her from accomplishing her dream of racing and completing the Iditarod.

From now on, Rita vowed silently, Mark was nothing more than the rival she'd originally seen him as and, despite her Aunt Julie's encouragement to be less severe with him, she wouldn't allow him even an inch into her life.

Mark was baffled by Rita's silent treatment. Just when he thought she was thawing a bit and starting to open up to him—bang! She always slammed the door in his face.

When they got back to Rita's house, Mark started to say something about it but Rita darted quickly from the truck and nearly ran into the house. What was with her, anyway?

Mark started unloading the supplies, and August soon came out to join him. August immediately noticed the furrows that lined Mark's forehead and knew the cause was most likely

Rita.

"You want to talk about it?" August asked, following Mark into the shed where they stored dog supplies.

"I suppose that would be the logical thing," Mark said, slamming a fifty-pound bag of commercial dog food to the ground. "However, I'm not feeling very logical. I'm confused and frustrated, but that's nothing unusual after spending the day with your daughter."

August grinned; he knew how infuriating Rita could be. "What happened?"

"I don't even know," Mark began. "She was reserved as always when we headed out but, by the time we got to Fairbanks, I thought she was starting to relax a bit. I figured on having a really nice trip home. You know, maybe talk through some of our feelings, but she was quieter than ever and never offered me so much as a single word."

August frowned and followed Mark to the truck. "She never said a word? She didn't even fight with you?"

"Nope," Mark replied and hoisted another bag of dog food on his shoulder.

"That's not like her," August said. "She must have it bad for you."

Mark nearly dropped the feed. "What? I just told you she wasn't even speaking to me. How can you say she has it bad for me?"

"Because Rita fights with people she doesn't care about. If the relationship isn't that important to her, she won't be put down, cast aside, or trod on in any manner. However, if she has feelings for you and the relationship is important to her, she handles it totally differently. Look at her and her mother. They scarcely share two words. Now, on occasion they will argue, but Rita hardly ever handles it in the same flippant manner she does when dealing with strangers," August stated. "Rita cares for you Mark, of this I'm certain. Her silence speaks more clearly than any words could."

"Then what do I do?" Mark asked seriously.

"Pray for her, Mark. Pray good and hard for her. I found the Bible open on her bed the other night. I think the Lord is really working her over and she needs to come to terms with Him first."

Mark nodded. "I'll pray."

ఇ

Inside the house, Rita found herself face-to-face with another mountain of emotion—her mother. Beth had purposefully sought out her daughter in order to take some measurements for Rita's insulated pants.

"Did you enjoy your time with Mark?" Beth asked innocently.

"Why?" Rita snapped, rather irritably. "Why do you ask that?"

"I just thought maybe, you and he—"

"Well, don't think about him and me," Rita interrupted. "There is nothing to think about. He's my trainer along with Dad, nothing more."

"You sound awfully firm on the matter," Beth said, taking the final measurement.

"I am," Rita replied. "Getting close to people only hurts you when they don't return your feelings."

eight

"I can't believe you sold them!" Rita nearly yelled the words. "How could you give up your Iditarod ingots, just to finance me in this race?"

"They weren't that important to me," August said with a shrug. "And I didn't think they were that important to anyone else."

Rita stomped her snowy boots against the straw-covered floor of her father's supply shed. "Well, they were to me," she finally said. She tried to ignore the fact that Mark was sitting not three feet away.

"Look, Rita," August began, "Mr. Simons wanted to make them into tourist necklaces. He paid me more than I deserved to be paid because he's a fair man and knows that by adding a simple silver chain to each, he'll net a small fortune. Added to that I sold four more dogs. Now we have enough money to travel in style and keep everyone fed and healthy. Don't begrudge me doing things my way, Rita. It's important for me to see you accomplish this. It may be your only chance to ever compete. Don't spoil it now."

Rita bit back a retort and nodded her head. "If that's what you want, Dad," she murmured.

"Good," August said with a smile. "We've got a lot of work to do and a great deal of information to go over. Mark, did you bring your notes on the trail?"

"Yup." Mark got to his feet, patting the pocket of his insulated overalls. "They're right here."

"Well, why don't we get started then. Let's go into the

office where it's warm," August suggested, and the other two followed at his lead.

Mark set aside his gloves and pulled a thick packet of papers from his pocket. Rita and her father joined him at the small table. "It's important to keep checking your list of supplies. You never know when you'll leave something out," Mark began the conversation.

Rita nodded and tried to quell the rapid beat of her heart when Mark gave her a quick wink.

"You know the mandatory items, but you've got important decisions to make about the rest of your gear. Most mushers on the Iditarod don't bother with the weight of a tent, they usually sleep on the sled or at one of the offered shelters—"

"If they sleep," August interrupted. "I don't imagine I got more than seven hours that first week."

Mark nodded and added with a laugh, "I think that's why they insist on the mandatory layovers. There's the twenty-four hour one that you must take at one time or another and a six-hour stop in White Mountain before the final push to Nome."

"Where do you take the twenty-four hour stop?" Rita asked.

"A lot of folks take it at Rohn," answered Mark. "You've just come through the mountains, and you're physically and emotionally drained. There's good shelter, food, and water there, and the people are great, too, but we're getting a little ahead of ourselves. First, you have to get that far."

"I'll get there," Rita said in a determined way that left both men little doubt that she would.

"There are other things to consider," Mark continued. "We'll head down to Anchorage in plenty of time to have the race-appointed veterinarians check out the dogs. You have to have all the shots up to date for parvo, rabies, and distemper."

"I have the records for all of that," August assured them. "You'll be given the Official Iditarod Cachet to carry with you. This is promotional material from the racing committee. It usually weighs about five pounds and has envelopes to be postmarked in Anchorage as well as Nome. It kind of celebrates the fact that the Iditarod trail is the old mail trail. The top finishers' envelopes are usually auctioned off to raise money for the race."

"Sounds like I'll have a crowded sled basket," muttered Rita.

"That's why what you choose to take along is so critical," Mark said, catching Rita's dark eyes. He wished silently that he could find some sign of closeness in them, but Rita was expert at masking her feelings, and he saw nothing. "You can always dump stuff off as you go, but you can't get what you need in the middle of the Alaskan Interior when you realize you've neglected to bring something."

"That's true," August stated. "I ran low on headlamp batteries early on and then I forgot to pack an extra pair of boots as well. When I got my only pair soaking wet and the wind chill made the temperatures seventy below zero, I knew I'd just cashed in the race."

Rita nodded, remembering how her father always reminded her to take extra boots whenever she and Mark trekked out into the wilds.

"Boots, extra clothes, batteries, light bulbs, gloves, ropes, harnesses, even sled runners are all things you'll have to choose carefully. You must also be able to transport any injured or ill dog on that sled and, in a pinch, sleep in it instead of on top of it. You have to be careful, and you have to be smart," Mark added.

Rita tried to absorb it all. She wanted very much to show both Mark and her father that she was fully capable of caring for herself. It was a dangerous position to put herself in, because with her prideful attitude, she purposefully avoided asking important questions, questions that could very well mean the difference between life and death.

"There are also rules of the road," Mark continued. "You'll get most of these on paper, but some are just givens. There's the Good Samaritan Rule that says no musher can be penalized for helping another musher in an emergency. You have to explain the incidents to the race official at the next checkpoint, but there shouldn't be any problems."

"Also, there are regulations related to the wildlife. If you have an incident arise where wildlife has attacked you, there are rules that relate to the situation. If the game is killed in defense of life or property, you are responsible to get that animal gutted and cared for," August remarked.

"But that could take a long time and by then you'd lose your place in the race," Rita said irritably. "That doesn't seem fair."

"No other musher can proceed ahead of you," Mark said, setting the record straight. "You don't lose your place." Was it Rita's imagination, or did Mark sound rather disgusted with her?

"If it's impossible to take care of the animal, for whatever reason," August continued, "you need to report the incident to the racing committee."

Rita nodded, still disturbed by Mark's intonation.

"Of course, we don't have to worry about cruelty to the animals," Mark began, "but rule number thirty of the Dog Procedures states that mushers aren't allowed to commit any action or inaction that causes preventable pain or suffering."

"And they are quite severe on this rule," August added. "Violation of this rule results in disqualification. The whole world watches the Iditarod with extreme concern for the health and safety of the animals. It's almost as if it doesn't matter what happens to the mushers as long as the dogs are pampered and cared for. Now, don't get me wrong," August continued, "I believe the dogs should always be cared for first. It's what I've taught you since you first started working with them. Your dogs are your life's blood out there. You feed them first, bed them down first, go over their bodies for injuries or problems, all before you take any form of personal comfort."

"I know all of that, Dad," Rita articulated.

"We're just trying to help you remember," Mark joined in. "There's so much that you must keep in mind." Mark noted the frown on Rita's face. "Look, Rita, no one is trying to make you feel stupid. We know that much of what you need to be aware of will come second nature to you. But, there will be those things that don't, and they'll probably be the very things that will not only make or break the race for you, but may result in a great many problems for you if you aren't on top of them."

"Okay. Okay," Rita retorted. "I'm all ears."

"Well, let's get on with the race itself," August suggested.

"That sounds good," Mark agreed. "Now first of all, is Anchorage to Eagle River. This is mostly urban and, as much as the dogs love to race, they hate the crowds and noise. There are hundreds of thousands of people, cars, helicopters, and above all else, noise. It makes the dogs jittery and the drivers tense. Fourth Street is where it all starts. At a banquet a couple of evenings before the race, you'll draw your starting position. Nine o'clock marks the ceremonial start of the race with the honorary number one musher sendoff. After that, the race officially begins at nine-o-two. Mushers will take off every two minutes after that and during the ride to Eagle River you'll carry a passenger."

"That's you, Daddy," Rita said, offering August a smile. August couldn't help but return his daughter's gesture.

"Who's riding with you, Mark?" August questioned.

"I have a friend in Anchorage and I've asked him to ride with me. It's kind of a pre-wedding present," Mark replied. "In fact, after the race, I'm going to be his best man."

"You never mentioned this, Mark," August commented with a quick glance at Rita. He noted the flash in her eyes that bespoke of sudden interest.

"I meant to. When I was arranging help for the kennel so that you and Beth could spend time in Anchorage, I arranged to cover the extra day I'd be away for the wedding. I was going to mention it to you the other day because I needed to pick up the wedding ring in Fairbanks, but you made it easy on me with that trip to town, and I just forgot."

Rita nearly fell off her chair. So the ring wasn't Mark's. This changed everything. But did she want it to? When she'd thought that Mark had someone else in his life, it was easier for Rita to separate her feelings from her thoughts.

Rita's reaction wasn't lost on August or Mark, but both men kept their thoughts to themselves, while Rita struggled just to hear what was being said about the trail.

❧

February came quickly to an end and Rita found herself on the way to Anchorage with her father. Her mother was coming down with Gerald and his wife in order to join in the festivities. After the Iditarod started, they would drive the dog vehicles to Eagle River where they would meet Rita and her team after the first leg of the race. At Eagle River, the dogs and sleds would be loaded into trucks and driven to Wasilla where the entire race would start again. The trail in earlier years passed over the mudflats of upper Cook Inlet to Knik. Due to the hazards of this area when unseasonable warmth left the ground and water unfrozen, the race was officially changed to restart in Wasilla.

The truck hit a series of bumps along a stretch of worn-out highway. Rita seemed not to notice. "I'm so excited, Dad."

"It only gets better," August said with a smile.

"I love the anticipation. Just knowing that something glorious like the Iditarod awaits is enough to keep me on the edge of my seat. I keep thinking of how it's going to be and even though I've never been there, you and Mark have made me feel as if I know how it will be," Rita chattered.

August nodded. "I'm glad you're excited. I knew you would be. You're finally realizing your dream and that's something quite special. I'm grateful to be a part of it before I die."

"Don't talk about dying, Daddy." Rita's voice betrayed her fear.

"Rita, you don't need to worry about me. I'm not afraid to die and when my time comes, I'll be ready. I guess my only real concern is whether or not you will be."

Rita swallowed hard. She thought of the verses her Aunt Julie had shared and all of her mother's speeches. Somehow those things were easier to deal with than her father's worries.

August tried not to notice the way Rita paled. Death, particularly the possibility of his death, caused Rita a great deal of fear. "Rita," he began gently, "you must let go of the fear you feel inside. Trust isn't an easy thing, but trust in God is something that will never let you down, because

God will never let you down."

"How can you be so sure?" Rita barely whispered the question.

"It's a matter of believing in the promises that God has given in the Bible, Rita. He said He'd never leave us and He never will."

"It's so hard," Rita replied. "The whole concept is difficult to believe. I mean, I see that God is real to you and Mom. I guess even Mark sees Him in a real way, but it just doesn't feel that way to me. I've prayed before, but I never felt as though my prayers went any farther than the room I was in. God just never made Himself very evident to me."

August nodded. "I can understand your predicament. I went through a time like that, too. Of course, you know all about that, and it isn't what's important right now. What is important is that you can have God in your life in a very real way. If you want Him, Rita, God will be there for you and He will help you to see Him."

"I'm afraid of trying." Rita's honest words hung in the air. "I mean it seems like everyone I've ever cared about has deserted me. Everyone, but you, that is."

"Do you really believe that?" August questioned.

"I don't know, Daddy. All I know is that ever since I was a little girl, I tried to understand why Mom felt so angry with me all the time and why none of my brothers or sisters seemed to have the time of day for me."

"Your brothers and sister were all so much older than you. You turned out to be a surprise gift from the Lord. You have to remember that you came nearly nine years after we presumed we were finished with diapers and bottles. Nevertheless, we loved you as much as any of the rest," August replied.

Rita shook her head. "No, I don't think so. You may

have felt that way, but Mother didn't. I overheard her tell Sarah that she'd never wanted me."

August looked stunned. "I find that hard to believe, Rita. I mean, I know the pregnancy was a shock to your mother and that we had to change a lot of plans, but I remember when she gave birth to you. I watched her nurse you. Your mother loved you as much as any of the others."

Rita winced and fell silent.

"Look, Rita," August said, dividing his concentration between the road and his daughter, "the issue here isn't the past, but the future. I'm going to pray that God will reveal Himself to you in a very real way and I'm going to pray that you can somehow get over your hurtful relationship with your mother and start over."

Rita looked out the window to avoid her father's face. She didn't want to appear vulnerable to his words, but the truth was, she felt compelled to listen.

"I mean it, Rita," August said in an authoritative voice. "I want you to figure out what the problem is between you and your mom and deal with it. I don't want to leave this world with the concern that either one of you is alone. I want you to be there for each other. I want you to love each other."

August's words hung on the air, stifling Rita into silent submission. "I want you to love each other," resounded in her mind as the forested miles of highway ticked by.

nine

The noise at the starting line on Fourth Street was intense and nerve-racking. Rita stood beside her dogs, soothing, quieting, and rechecking every harness and line. She could feel the adrenaline surging through her veins, making her heart pound hard against her temples.

Mentally, she made a list of the items she'd packed and one by one she went over them. With each crunch of snow beneath her heavy boots, Rita felt the urge to be off, building inside.

Dandy gave a whimpered howl that was quickly followed by howls from the other dogs. Rita saw her father lean over and give the lead dog a quick pat on the head. She thought he whispered something to the dog, but found a tap on her shoulder distracted her from finding out what it was that August had said.

"Yes?" She whirled around to find Mark's intense eyes. His cheeks were red from the wind, but his expression of excitement matched her own.

"Are you ready, Texas Rita?" Mark asked in puffs of icy air. Rita couldn't help but grin. "I feel like I've worked a lifetime to get here."

"You have worked hard," Mark agreed. "I'm proud of the way you put aside our differences."

Rita prickled at Mark's words. "I don't know what you're talking about."

Mark laughed. "You weren't the most cooperative student as I recall."

Rita started to answer but found her reply interrupted by one of the race officials.

"I'm here to mark your dogs," he told her as he moved with paint to dab on each dog's fur for purposes of identification. This would prevent the switching of dogs while out on the trail. Rita anticipated this from things her father and Mark had told her, still she didn't like anyone else handling her dogs.

She followed the man in silence, however, her mind still on Mark's words. *Forget about him,* she chided her heart and mind. *You don't need him or anyone else.* Yet even as she tried to convince herself of this, her father's words of salvation and heavenly security kept pounding at her.

By the time the official moved on, Rita found Mark gone as well. August came up with a grin a mile wide.

"Okay Number Nineteen," he said referring to the number Rita had drawn for her position in the start of the Iditarod, "it won't be long now."

"I know," Rita mumbled.

"What's wrong?" August asked suddenly concerned.

"Umm? Oh, nothing," Rita said, noting her father's worried look. She wanted to assure him but, in order to keep her guard up, she also needed to distance herself. "It's just jitters, Dad."

"I understand. Look, we're going to be taking off shortly. Do you have everything?" August asked.

"I think so," Rita answered. "Where's Mom and Gerald?"

"Oh, they're out there, somewhere. Don't you worry about them. They'll be there at Eagle River waiting with the dog trucks."

"Well, I guess that's all I can ask," Rita said with a hesitant smile.

"Don't worry," August said as he patted his daughter's

hand. "Everything will be fine once the race starts."

Rita wanted to believe that, but in her heart she knew the turmoil was much more than the race.

⋇

"One more, Rita," August called from the sled basket. "One more racer and then we're off."

Rita said nothing, her mind was a blur of fanatical fans waving and yelling their support. Where in the world had all those people come from? There were television cameras and reporters everywhere, not to mention five blocks of colorful, screaming people and extremely bright lights.

The next thing Rita knew was the numbing grip of her hand on the sled handle and the pounding of her heart in her ears.

"Nineteen—go!" the announcer called.

"Dandy, hike!" Rita yelled above the crowd's roar. Dandy led the pack of dogs without need of encouragement. The team was in a near frenzy as they shot down the street.

Rita knew nothing but the feel of the dogs and the frosty air against her cheeks. The sounds were all muted in her head while the faces blended into one.

I'm really doing it! Rita thought. *I'm finally racing the Iditarod!*

The race trail headed down Cordova Hill, with a spectacular view of downtown Anchorage. Rita worked to slow the team as they plunged down the slope, but the dogs were as excited as she was. It was exhilarating and no one wanted to slow down for any reason.

The next miles followed inner-city trails where people still cheered the mushers on. It wasn't until the trail finally began to parallel the Glenn Highway that the people thinned to sporadic gatherings.

"Isn't this great!" August yelled over his shoulder.

"Yes," Rita replied. "It's everything I knew it would be."

August laughed heartily. "You ain't seen nothing yet, kid. Hang on for Act Two. It's a doosey!"

Amidst the noise of people and crowds, Rita worked hard to keep the team under control. Each time they approached an intersection, traffic was stopped from all directions while her team moved through, but the honking of zealous fans and general pandemonium made driving the team a tiresome task.

Rita had hoped to think through her anger and frustration on the trail, but if the run from Anchorage to Eagle River was any indication of how her time would be spent, there wouldn't be much time for thinking.

Two hours and eighteen minutes later, without a single mishap, Rita and August passed under the banner welcoming them to Eagle River.

"Good time, Rita," August said as they checked in.

Rita nodded and looked around for Mark. He'd left a good ten places behind her, but that didn't mean a great deal. She'd no sooner cast a squinted stare at the horizon when she caught sight of him. He was making incredible time.

August spotted him about the same time. "I bet he'll be under two hours!" The excitement in August's voice left a jealous mark on Rita's heart.

Mark came flying across the trail and clocked in at one hour and fifty-eight minutes. While August stomped off through the snow to congratulate his partner, Rita cooled her heels and unharnessed her dogs.

"You did well, Rita," her brother said as he came to help her with loading the animals.

"Thanks, Gerald. It's good to see you again," she answered rather mechanically, not really meaning a word she said. Rita knew it wasn't fair to take out her fury on Gerald, but she ignored her pang of conscience and kept her distance.

"Rita!" Beth called as she got out of the pickup. "What was your time?"

"Two-eighteen," Rita replied, surprised at her mother's enthusiasm.

"Fantastic!" Beth stepped forward and hugged her daughter. She laughed as she pulled away from Rita. "There's so much padding to you, I'm not at all convinced that you're really under all of that," she said pointing to Rita's insulated coveralls.

Rita laughed in spite of herself. She'd never seen her mother so happy, especially when it involved Rita. Surprisingly enough it was her father who spoiled Rita's moment of happiness.

"Mark did it in an hour and fifty-eight minutes!" said August. "Can you believe it, Beth?"

"That's great," Beth agreed. "I'm so proud of Rita and Mark. They've done really well, haven't they?" It was more a statement than a question.

"They certainly have," August said. "Now we need to get these animals loaded up and move up to Wasilla."

Rita felt disappointed in the lack of fanfare from her father. Somehow she'd presumed he'd been her biggest fan, not her mother. Putting it behind her, Rita knew she'd have plenty of time to contemplate it on the way to Wasilla.

❧

The next day the whole thing started all over. This time Rita waited behind while Mark disappeared down the trail. In her mind was the overwhelming drive to beat his time and win the race.

For all the truly important reasons, Wasilla was where the Iditarod really began. The race restarted with the biggest difference being that this time the mushers went out alone. Rita refused to even look back when her time came. When the signal was given, she steadied herself behind the sled and ran for all she was worth.

The first one hundred miles out of Wasilla was called "Moose Alley" and for a good reason. It was here that the race trail passed through an area where large numbers of moose spent the winter. When the snow became too deep for the moose to find food, they often took to the roadways, railroad tracks, and any place else that had been cleared of the blanket of white.

Rita kept alert for any interference and, in the process, passed two other teams who were already experiencing problems. She was out less than four hours, when the snow began to fall. At first the flakes came down in gentle flurries but within a matter of several miles the conditions had built into a full-fledged blizzard. Rita come upon four teams who had backtracked their way in order to relocate the trail and, rather than lose her place and assure everyone they were headed in the right direction, Rita took a gamble and headed on.

The gamble paid off and Rita soon found one of the trail markers. "Good," she said aloud, adrenaline racing through her system. "I've moved out ahead of six teams already. If I'm just willing to take a few chances, I can win this race!"

When the snow let up a bit, Rita knew it would be a good time to rest the dogs. She pulled off the trail and dug out dried fish for each of the team. She felt hot inside her multiple layers of clothing and it was then that she realized the temperatures were warming.

Glancing around her, Rita could see a clearing in the skies

up ahead and bright sunlight filtering through the sporadic cloud coverage. The snow had stopped falling altogether, but the trail had been partially obliterated by the storm. In the far distance, Rita thought she heard dogs barking. Her pulse began to race. "I can't lose ground, now."

Rita resecured the sled cargo, shed her heavy parka, and pulled on a beaver fur hat that her mother had made for her as a Christmas gift. She pulled sunglasses from a pouch near the handle bar, stuffed them in her insulated coveralls, and pressed the dogs forward.

Rita believed luck was with her as the skies cleared and the trail markers appeared faithfully. She urged the dogs to go faster and faster, but they slowed as the trail grew mushy from the sun's warmth.

Rethinking her strategy, Rita reasoned that waiting for sunset might be better for her time and the dog's health. She drove them another couple of hours and finally located a place near a stream. Her mind whirled as she rationalized her decision.

"Everyone will be slowed down by the thawing trail," she spoke to herself. "No one will make good time and if I stop now, rest and feed the dogs and take a nap myself, we'll be able to push through all night." It was sensible, but with each team that passed her, Rita felt the urge to get back behind the sled and join them.

Instead, Rita built a fire and heated food for the dogs. After seeing each of them fed and bedded down, she pulled out her heavy snow parka and laid down on top of her sled. Setting the alarm on her watch for four o'clock, Rita placed the timepiece in her fur hat so that it was right up against her ear. Then, pulling the parka over her body and face, Rita slept.

Again the gamble paid off. When Rita awoke, the sunlight was fading and the trail was already growing firm again. After making sure to water the dogs one more time to keep them from trying to eat snow on the trail, Rita mushed out for her next checkpoint—Skwenta, Alaska.

When she arrived at the checkpoint, most of the teams had been there far ahead of her. Some of the drivers were giving their dogs extra rest, but as soon as Rita checked in she felt like hitting the trail again. The Delia House, long known for its hospitality, held a welcome aroma of chili, stews, and freshly brewed coffee.

Rita sat down nervously to a bowl of beef stew and bread while she mentally calculated who was who and what kind of time they must have maintained. She gulped the food down and while most of the other drivers went to sleep, Rita donned her parka again and went back to her dogs.

The one thing she hadn't counted on was a deluge of reporters. Flashbulbs went off making the dogs nervous and blinding Rita.

"You're not pushing out again are you?" one reporter asked and thrust a tape recorder in front of Rita.

"Y-yes," Rita stammered and tried to shield her eyes from the television camera lights that were added to the flashing lights.

"The other drivers are giving their dogs a longer rest, aren't you concerned that your dogs will be overworked?" a woman interviewer questioned. "I thought there were strict rules about the dogs."

"I rested early in the day when the trails were mushy. My dogs are fine," Rita replied in clipped tones that betrayed her agitation. "Now, if you'll excuse me."

Rita hurried to leave the checkpoint and after meeting all her obligations, quickly found her way down the trail and headed for Finger Lake.

In the bright moonlinght, the trail was easy enough. The stars filled the skies overhead and Rita thought she'd never know anything as beautiful. Following the Skwenta River, Rita calculated that Finger Lake was some forty-five miles away. She knew she'd have to rest the dogs for short spells before then, but Finger Lake would represent her next major stop.

Silently, she watched the miles pass by. She saw the heavy cloud bank that edged its way across the western skies, while over her right shoulder northern lights danced in the March sky. What a land of contrast!

Lowlands gave way to foothills and foothills passed into the mighty Alaskan Range but, even though each passing mile offered more difficult obstacles, one thought haunted Rita's mind—*Where was Mark and what kind of time was he keeping?*

ten

The following day wasn't quite as warm, but Rita repeated her system between intermittent snows. She knew that other mushers were following the same plan and she kept moving as quickly as possible to gain distance.

True to what her father and Mark had told her, she couldn't count more than a few hours of sleep in total. The lack of sleep didn't discourage her, however. Rita kept reminding herself of how easy the trail had been so far and despite her desperate need for sleep, she kept to her self-appointed schedule.

"I've taken chances," she said aloud, "but they've paid off and I know they were the right things to do."

Rita smiled to herself as the dogs moved at a steady lope. At Finger Lake she'd moved up nine places and after an uneventful roller coaster ride through Happy River Gorge, Rita was beginning to feel smug in her self-confidence. "I knew I didn't need anybody," she reminded herself. The cold wind made her cheekbones numb, but she didn't care. She knew she could win the race.

In the back of her mind, August's words mingled with her self-assured thoughts. Her father said she needed God and no matter how she tried to deny Him, Rita knew it was true. That was the biggest problem about all the miles of solitude on the trail—it gave a person too much time to think.

Rita thought about stopping the dogs in order to get her headphones. Maybe listening to some of her favorite music would help her to keep her conscience in check. She glanced at her watch and decided against it. She could just as well block out the thoughts by forcing her interests elsewhere. At least she hoped she could.

The dogs were holding up well and each checkpoint had shown them to be in excellent shape despite the way Rita pushed them. It was Rita who suffered. At times she thought she imagined teams just ahead of her but when she rubbed her eyes with the back of her mittens, the images faded. It wasn't until Rita thought the dog sled was floating up into the air that she decided to rest. Rohn was only a few hours ahead of her and both Mark and her father had suggested she spend her twenty-four-hour layover here. All she had to do was hold on until Rohn.

While Rohn and a good night's sleep waited just down the trail, Rita knew she would still have to face the challenge of Dalzell Gorge. Her father had described this stretch of the Iditarod as a nightmare.

First, there was the climb from Puntilla Lake to 3,200-foot Rainy Pass. The dogs had managed this with relative ease and Rita was beginning to think they were living a charmed life. Maybe her father had just been overly tired by the time he'd come this far, she surmised. Maybe it was just that he was so much older when he'd run the race.

As the team crossed over the divide, Rita had to turn her full attention to the trail at hand. The path ahead plunged into a steep, winding trail that moved rapidly downhill at a rate of about one thousand feet in little more than five miles.

Rita clung to the bar and rode the brake constantly to counter the dog's continued slipping. At one point she saw Dandy go down and slide several feet. Over and over the dogs recovered their falls while Rita found herself near to prayer for the safety of the team.

Things went better for several minutes and Rita breathed

a sigh of relief. She tried to get her bearings on the situation, feeling her pulse racing wildly. Ahead of her, the narrow canyon was lined with boulders and crossed several ice bridges that spanned partially frozen creeks. If the dogs lost their footing while traveling over the bridges, they could send the entire team, sled, and all, into the water below. Rita couldn't afford to lose the time, nor would she endanger the dogs.

"Dandy, whoa!" she called and held the brake tight to bring the dogs to a near stop.   Easing them forward, Rita held her breath with each crossing and didn't let it out until they'd safely reached the opposite side.

"Just get us to Rohn," Rita murmured, uncertain to whom she was speaking. "We'll be fine if we can just to Rohn."

❧

The shelter cabin at Rohn waited as official Iditarod Checkpoint Number Eight. Rita dragged into the clearing running behind the sled on nothing but sheer determination. She was now two hundred seventy-five miles from Anchorage and, while the halfway mark was still to be reached, Rita was simply grateful for having made it this far.

Coming to a halt, Rita was quickly surrounded by people. One by one she answered questions and even signed an autograph book, before the crowd dispersed and left her to work.

"I see you're still in one piece." It was Mark.

Rita cast a weary glance upward from where she had bent down to check over her dogs. "You, too," was all that squeaked out.

"You gonna layover here?" Mark asked sympathetically.

"Yes." Rita straightened out and nearly fell over.

"Easy," Mark said, reaching out to steady her.

"I'm fine, really," Rita answered and tried to push away.

"I have to log in and let them know I'm staying." She started to walk away, but turned back around. "What about you?"

"I'll be leaving in a few hours," Mark replied. The concern he held for Rita was evident in his expression.

"You're that far ahead of me?"

"Is that all that concerns you?" Mark asked a bit sarcastically.

Rita rolled her neck to relieve the strain. "It isn't everything, but it's important."

Mark shook his head as Rita moved off to speak to the officials. He knew it was difficult to truly enjoy the race while you were running it, but in Rita's case it was even worse. She was all driving competition and no pleasure. The fire of that drive was clear in her eyes, in spite of her exhaustion.

Rita tried to ignore the way Mark stared after her. She met her race responsibilities, picked up supplies, and moved away from the shelter area to bed down with the dogs.

"The wind's due to pick up tonight," Mark said from somewhere behind her.

Rita turned wearily to find him toting a bale of straw. "What are you doing?"

"Just bringing the dogs some bedding." His casual reply left Rita no room to protest.

"What's the temperature?" she asked instead and reached into her pocket for a knife to cut the bailing wire.

"Thirty below and dropping. When that wind comes down the pass, it's going to feel like a hundred below. I'd climb in that sled and in my sleeping bag if I were you," Mark answered.

"Just put the bale here," she motioned. "I'm going to stake out the dogs and then I'll distribute the straw." Mark dropped the bale and stood back wishing he could do more to ease Rita's exhaustion. He knew she needed to do everything for herself, but he also knew her pride wouldn't allow her to think rationally.

"May I keep you company while you get the dogs fed and watered?" he questioned.

"I guess so," Rita said and moved painfully slowly to position her dogs.

No other conversation passed between them until after Rita had a hearty fire roaring. She thawed rich mixtures of commercial dog food, liver, chicken, and salmon to feed the dogs, then melted snow and poured water for each one until she was certain they'd had their fill. Mark made conversation that was solely responsible for keeping Rita on her feet, but she never would have admitted his help.

"You gonna eat?" Mark asked when he saw that Rita was finished with the dogs.

"No," she sighed. A gust of wind blew through the trees just then. "It's getting colder and I'm going to sleep. Will I see you when I wake up?"

"I doubt it. You won't surface dreamland for ten or twelve hours if my guess is right. I'll be gone in two."

Rita nodded. She wanted to ask him about his time, but her mind begged for sleep. "I'll see you when you cross the finish line in Nome, then." Her reply amused Mark.

"Not likely, Eriksson. Not likely."

Rita watched Mark walk away. She hadn't realized how comforting his presence was until he stood in the lighted doorway of the Bureau of Land Management cabin and turned to offer her a wave before going inside.

Stripping off her parka and wet coveralls, Rita quickly pulled the sleeping bag around her and nuzzled down into the sled basket. She wiggled around to work the sled cover up over her before burying her head inside the sleeping bag.

The warmth eased her aching muscles and sleep was immediate. For the first time in days, Rita gave in to the demands of her body.

❧

When Rita awoke nine hours later she could hear the wind howling from outside her sled bag. She pulled her wrist watch to her face and hit the light button to reveal the date and time. Seeing that she was still early into her twenty-four hours, Rita allowed herself to linger in the warmth.

Licking her lips slowly, Rita realized for the first time how cracked and dried they were. Water sounded even better than food and her stomach was protesting quite loudly for that substance. It was a difficult choice. Food and water or restful warmth?

Finally choosing the food, Rita pushed back the basket cover and peered out. During the night, the winds had brought snow and buried the dogs and the basket in an insulation of white. Rita pulled her frozen coveralls on and secured her parka, while Dandy lazily peeked blue eyes out from where his bushy tail covered his muzzle.

"Well, boy," Rita called out. "What do you think? Are we going to win this race?" Dandy whimpered, then yipped. "I'll take that as a yes," Rita answered and went to work melting snow.

By the time Rita's layover was completed, the wind had picked up to forty-miles an hour and the temperature registered at forty-five below. Thick heavy snow clouds hung in a gray lifeless form over the entire area. There would be little, if any, light today, Rita surmised.

She quickly harnessed the dogs and stood ready to leave when her official twenty-four hours was up. It was almost like starting the race again. The dogs were refreshed, well fed and watered, and eager for the trail. They lived to do this work and they loved it. Rita smiled as she stroke Dandy one last time, remembering a woman in Anchorage who thought it cruel that Rita raced her dogs. The woman couldn't understand. She saw the harnesses of confinement and the weight of the load. What she didn't see was the animation in the dogs, their yips of enthusiasm, their jumps of excitement. Nor did this woman know of the dogs left behind to howl and mourn their misfortune. It was all a matter of how one looked at the situation.

Something in Rita's heart took notice at that thought. Her mother's indifference came to mind. Rita frowned at the memory and quickly brushed it aside. A matter of perspective or not, Rita had a race to run and now wasn't the time for soul searching. Or was it?

❧

The trail was firm beneath her feet as Rita ran behind her sled. The dogs, ever faithful to their job, kept a steady lope as they moved out of the Rohn area and past the Kuskokwim River's south fork. Rita had been thoroughly warned about the trail to come. She would soon be passing into the Fare-well Burn. This 360,000-acre area of tundra and spruce forests had been destroyed many years prior in a forest fire. It left behind an obstacle course of fallen trees and regrowth of sedge-tussock tundra. The tussock, clumps of grass that mushroomed out two feet high or more, froze solid in the winter and presented rock-solid opposition to the mushers of the Iditarod. Many a driver had been injured, some even seriously, when their sleds and teams had run up against the tussock.

Rita calculated the checkpoints to come. There would be Nikolai first, then McGrath, Takotna, and finally Ophir. Ophir was where the trail would separate and take the southerly route and pass through Iditarod and it was Iditarod that represented the halfway mark. It seemed like a whole world away.

⋇

The hours rushed by and the distance passed, too. Rita had found the "Burn" painfully tedious and slow. Snow made visibility difficult but, one by one, Rita located the trail markers and pressed on. The checkpoints passed quickly and with them came the cultural change from areas that had been heavily influenced by the whites, to lands primarily settled with native Athapaskan Indians.

She was greeted enthusiastically at Nikolai, finding herself in fifth position, but still behind Mark. The villagers had greeted each arriving team with shouts of praise and welcome. A huge bonfire had been built for the purpose of heating water for the dogs and the school had been dismissed to allow the children to run from team to team seeking autographs.

Rita was given a hot meat sandwich that she quickly wolfed down before pushing on. Leaving a single sled team behind while the driver changed runners, Rita pushed ahead for McGrath.

By nightfall she'd made Takotna. This river town had served as a landing and supply center during the gold rush days in Alaska. Now only numbering around fifty in population, Rita was welcomed every bit as heartily as she had been in Nikolai. She'd never seen so much food in all her life and graciously ate her fill after seeing to it that her team ate first.

The snow fell heavier still as she mushed out to reach Ophir. More than one native encouraged her to stay on in Takotna until the storm abated, but Rita was feverish with the thought of passing Mark.

It was the endless miles of darkness that gave Rita too

much time to think. "If I can only make it to Iditarod first," she whispered to the night skies, "I could win the silver ingots and give them to Dad." There are only five teams in front of me and one of them is Mark, she thought to herself and disregarded the beliefs that being the first one to reach the halfway point jinxed you from winning the race. She knew that only once had the midway winner gone on to win the Iditarod, but she simply didn't care. She wished there were someway to slow down the other mushers.

When she finally arrived in Ophir, amidst near-blizzard conditions, Rita felt as though she'd been granted her wish. All five of the teams ahead of her, including Mark's, were still there.

Mark met her and noted the frenzied excitement in her eye. "The weather's too bad to push ahead," Mark commented as Rita's team approached him. "We've decided to hold up a spell."

"Have they put a freeze on the race?" Rita questioned, feeling her fervor fade.

"No," Mark replied. "We just know what these storms are like. It'll blow over in a short time and we can be off then. There's no use in risking life and limb."

"I can't believe you're all afraid to mush out in this," Rita said, waving her hand. "I've come the last twenty miles in this storm and, while cold and extremely frustrating, it's not worth stopping for."

"You don't mean that you plan to move on out in it?" Mark's question fanned the flame of Rita's pride.

"I certainly do. As soon as I get the team cared for, we're out of here." She hurried off before Mark could say anything to stop her. There was a chance to win the ingots. There was a chance to win the race!

eleven

"I don't want you to go, Rita," Mark stated. He put his hand out to take hold of Dandy's harness. "I owe it to your father to keep you from risking your life out there."

Rita's eyes blazed holes in Mark's heart. "Let go of my dogs. It's my choice to run, just as it was your choice to stay. My father isn't out here running this race, I am. Now let me go."

Mark dropped the harness and took hold of Rita with both hands. "It's suicide to go any farther," Mark tried to reason. "If you don't care about your family, I do. I don't want to have to explain to them how I allowed you to go out and become the first human life lost in the entire history of the Iditarod."

"I never asked you to babysit me," Rita said in a surprisingly calm tone.

"I just care about you, Rita. Think about it. I think I've proven it enough times. It's not just August and Beth. I care about what happens to you."

Rita felt her resolve giving way; her eyes softened for a moment before she shrugged away from Mark's hold. "I don't want you to care," she whispered and walked back to the sled. She gave a soft whistle barely heard through the wind, but it was enough that Dandy's sensitive ears picked it up and then they were gone.

Mark kicked at the snow and muttered all the way back to where his team was contently curled up beneath the snow. He began to ready his sled without real thought to what he was doing, but in his heart he knew that he'd have to follow Rita. He'd never forgive himself if something happened to her.

"Williams!" a voice sounded above the wind. "Where are you going?" It was one of the checkpoint officials.

"I'm heading out for Iditarod," Mark replied.

"I can't let you go," the man returned. "They've put a freeze on the race. Can't get supplies flown up to the next checkpoints because of the blizzard. Until they can, the race stops."

"But Rita Eriksson just left a few minutes ago. She'll be out there all alone if I don't follow her," Mark protested even knowing how foolish his argument sounded.

"Sorry, Williams. She took off before the word came down, but if you head out you'll be breaking the rules." The man saw the look of concern on Mark's face. "It shouldn't be a long wait. Try not to worry."

❧

But it was a long wait and team after team mushed into Ophir only to be told they had to stay put until supplies could be sent on ahead. Most took the opportunity to sleep or repair their sleds, but Mark paced and fretted until he was nearly sick from the thought of Rita meeting with an accident.

"Lord," Mark found himself praying, "I don't understand what gets into that woman, but I care for her in a way I wasn't sure I could ever care for another human being. Lord, I don't want her to die and yet. . . ." His words trailed into silence as he remembered a sermon he'd once heard about people thwarting God's efforts to work in the lives of rebellious souls. "God, I don't want to interfere in Your plans for Rita. Go with her and help me to leave it in Your hands, Amen."

The prayer made Mark feel marginally better, but when one day passed into two and the checkpoint official gave him the news that Rita had never made it to Iditarod, Mark could stand it no longer.

"I have to go after her!" he said as he readied his dogs.

"You'll just get yourself killed," the official told him. "Or, you'll be disqualified from the race."

"I don't care. I'm a certified search and rescue team member, I can't just sit here knowing that she's out there somewhere in this storm. I have to try to find her, or I'm afraid she's not going to come out of this alive. Do you really want to be the one remembered for keeping a musher from being saved?"

"I'll send out other people," the man replied. "I assure you, Miss Eriksson will be located as soon as possible, but I can't risk the lives of ten other people because of the foolish gamble of one racer."

"I'm not asking you to," Mark said, taking hold of the sled bar. "I'll gladly give my own life for hers."

The man's face change from angry frustration to confused. Mark took the man's silence as a form of understanding and mushed the dogs out into the storm.

ã

Rita knew she was hopelessly lost. She hadn't been able to locate a marker or tag of any kind and the trail was long since obliterated.

The blizzard raged on around her making it impossible to care for the dogs or even set up a proper camp. The few times she'd tried, she'd failed miserably and struggled to push on. When the wind let up a bit, she strained to hear the sounds of civilization. Nothing came back to her ears but the death-like silence. Exhaustion hung round her like a mantle of fur.

"I've got to make camp. I've got to rest," she said aloud. The dogs were wearing out fast and Rita knew she was pushing them dangerously close to dehydration and death.

Feeling her way along the team, Rita checked the dogs' feet. She needed to change the booties on two of dogs' paws. She hated this job that, even under good circumstances, was difficult to do. Each dog represented four booties and four dancing paws and Rita would have to discard her mittens and gloves because it was impossible to put the tiny socks on and get the closures secured through padded fingers.

The exposure to windchills of minus one hundred degree could freeze flesh in a matter of seconds and Rita knew the only way to combat the cold would be to pull her gloves off and on for each bootie.

"This isn't fair," she screamed to the howling wind. "I deserve to win this race. I've taken the chances. I've sacrificed my comfort. Why are You against me, God?"

A blast of wind slammed into Rita knocking her into the team. The dogs yipped and tangled, while she fought the harnesses and lines to recover from the fall. She felt tears form and just as quickly they froze to her lashes and burned her eyes.

"What is it You want of me, Lord? I can't go back. I can't go forward. If You won't help me," Rita moaned, "why must You hurt me?"

Rita crawled on her hands and knees to get back to the sled basket. Each inch covered was filled with pain but Rita was determined to make it. She managed to open the covering even though she couldn't see it through the snow and her painful eyes.

Now the worst was upon her. Rita knew she would have to shed her wet clothes if she was to ever gain warmth in her sleeping bag. With nearly frozen fingers, Rita placed her mittens inside the basket and worked her way out of the layers of clothes. At the first possible moment, she scurried into the sleeping bag and snuggled down into the basket.

·∾·

Mark knew his plan was foolish, yet he also knew he maintained an edge of experience that Rita didn't have. He and his team had been in situations like this before and would no doubt be in them again.

Wind and snow pelted them as Mark led the team forward at a steady walk. Moving slowly and working his way diligently, Mark managed to find the first marker without too much difficulty. He reassured the dogs with praise and pressed on, all the while he looked for anything that would indicate that Rita had passed through the same area.

Pausing in the storm, Mark lifted up a prayer. "Please Lord, help me in this search. You know where Rita is and You can guide me to her. Please abate this storm, in the name of Jesus. Amen."

Mark kept moving. Through the blowing snow he constantly had to break trail for the dogs. He felt the exhaustion of hours spent in snowshoes rapidly draining his strength. Just when he thought he'd have to turn back, a miracle happened—the snow stopped.

"Thanks, God," Mark whispered under his breath.

·∾·

Rita finally felt her body begin to thaw and, with the warmth, she was able to think more clearly. Her first order of business had to be caring for the dogs. She could hear the wind howling outside the sled basket, in fact it rocked the sled as she lay inside. No doubt the dogs had curled up to sleep and were now buried beneath a layer of snow, oblivious to the perils at hand. Rita wished silently that she could be as incognizant.

Shifting her weight, Rita pushed back her fur hat and moaned. A painful knot had formed on her forehead from where she'd hit it when the wind knocked her to the ground. Rita knew she wasn't seriously wounded, but her head was pounding as her body warmed.

"I guess my charmed portion of the trip is over," Rita mused. She tried to encourage her weary heart, but it was difficult at best. Were she in the habit of prayer, she might consider talking things over with God, but that wasn't her style. In the back of her mind, however, Rita couldn't help but think of a hundred different Bible stories where people found themselves facing problems and hardships. Memory verses from childhood reminded her of their commitment to God and how they cried out to Him when they were in trouble.

"Mother would like this," Rita laughed. "She's always pushing God at me. Now here I am in the middle of Alaska, in a blizzard, without a clue as to where I am, and all I can focus on is how God helped people in the Bible."

Rita felt the sled still and the wind grow calm. The storm was finally abating and Rita knew it was time to get to work. Pushing out of her cocoon, she crawled from the basket and surveyed the damage.

Dry, drifting snow still swirled in tiny whirlwinds around the sled, while Rita pulled on her insulated clothes and went into action to get a fire going. The exhausted dogs barely stirred, although Dandy raised his head to give Rita an appraising look before going back to sleep.

Within an hour she had food and water for both the dogs and herself. The skies overhead had cleared to a pale, powder blue and even with the sun hanging above the southern horizon, there was little warmth. At least Rita could get her bearings now and hopefully relocate the trail. Her optimism returned and her heart grew lighter. The dogs, sensing the change in their mistress, grew excited again. They were pacing and yipping and Rita knew they were ready to be back on the trail. But where was the trail?

Rita pulled on her snowshoes and led the dogs out. There was no clear direction that beckoned Rita more than another. She looked for anything that might indicate civilization or symbolize a connection with the Iditarod race, but there wasn't anything. She pulled out her compass and depended on it alone to guide her in a direction that would lead them to safety.

Hours later, the biggest mistake Rita had made was, once again, ignoring the weather. The snow moved in from the west and with it came the wind.

Old snow blew with the new, and soon, Rita found it again impossible to see. The dogs whined and slowed and Rita felt her courage slipping away. She halted the team and tied a rope to the sled and to herself. Using her headlamp, Rita left the dogs behind and ventured ahead to find some sign of shelter.

"I can't give up," she said even though she knew she was now several days behind the other teams. She had no way of knowing that the other racers had just been allowed to leave Ophir.

Finding nothing to aid her on her way, Rita turned around and headed back to the dogs. She retraced her steps following the rope and then she felt her heart skip a beat. The rope had come untied; the sled was nowhere in sight!

twelve

Cold permeated the insulation of Rita's coveralls. She stomped aimlessly through the blowing snow, watching, calling, and hoping.

"Dandy!" she yelled at the top of her lungs, but the wind muted the sound even as the word left her lips.

The dogs were nowhere to be found and visibility was impossible. Rita knew the seriousness of the circumstances. Without the dogs she would most likely die!

"I have to keep moving," she reasoned. "I'll freeze to death if I stand here and wait." She thought of building a shelter with the snow. Her Aunt Julie told her that once such a shelter had saved her life. Rita remembered that her Aunt Julie had survived two days just off the Bering Sea in a haven she'd built with her own hands out of snow and ice.

"No!" Rita spoke aloud. "I'll find the dogs. Dandy would never have left without me." But, even as she said the words, Rita knew it was improbable that the team was awaiting her return.

Step after step, Rita forced herself forward. Her feet were beginning to ache and her legs were cramping from the strain. It was fast becoming a hopeless situation.

After what seemed hours, Rita was ready to face the facts. "I'm not going to make it," she whispered. "I'm going to die out here doing the one thing I dreamed a lifetime of doing. All I wanted was to race the Iditarod and now it's going to kill me."

But running the race wasn't all, Rita's conscience quickly

reminded her. Winning the race was what you planned on. Winning was so important that you ignored the advice of seasoned racers, people who knew the trail and have more experience than you could ever hope to have.

"I've been extremely foolish," Rita said and stumbled forward another step. Her thick boot caught the edge of a fallen tree and sent her sprawling, face down, onto the snowy ground.

Why get up? She challenged herself to find a reason to go on. There was none. "This is God's punishment for ignoring Him and turning away from my mother," she announced. She had never felt so alone.

The thought of her mother made Rita's heart ache. All her life she'd wanted to feel close to Beth and in spite of the times Rita had determined to put her hurts aside, inevitably, she added another brick to the wall between them.

"When times are difficult and you are most alone," her mother had told her, "God is no farther away than a whispered prayer."

The wind lessened and with it the snow, but Rita couldn't see anything but white. A whispered prayer came to Rita's mind, but not of her own making. The prayer she remembered was one from her childhood memories. It was her mother's prayer at Rita's bedside that came to mind. "Father, this child was given to me from You and by Your love, I give her back. Watch over her, Father, as only You can, and help her to know Your voice when You call her."

Such a sweet, yet simple prayer, Rita thought and the memory warmed her. Nothing to offend or harm, only a mother's desire for her child to know God. The memory wasn't painful, it was pleasant and Rita wondered silently how she could have allowed such hatred to grow against others, especially her mother.

Rita struggled to sit up and pulled her knees tightly to her chest. "I'm afraid to die," she whispered. "I know the truth, just like mother said. I know what God did for me by sending his Son, Jesus, to die for me. I've always wanted God to somehow make Himself real to me. Yet, even sitting here waiting to die, He still doesn't seem real and I'm not convinced He'd listen to me even if I whispered that prayer." Absentmindedly, Rita began packing snow around herself to form a shelter.

Mark saw the reprieve in the storm as a godsend, but he also noticed the heavy clouds that pushed in from the west. The air was strangely still around him and Mark found the silence almost hypnotic.

He urged his team forward, but knew he'd lost track of the trail marker's some time back. "God give me the wisdom to find my way through this. Guide me to find Rita and safety, Amen."

Just then a blurred image in the distance came into focus. It was a dog team. No, Mark realized as he squinted his eyes, it was Rita's dog team!

Having worked with those dogs since they were pups, Mark gave Dandy a whistle that the dog instantly recognized. "Here Dandy, come," Mark's authoritative voice called.

Dandy perked his ears and heeded the command. Mark anchored his own team and stomped across the frozen ground to retrieve Rita's team. He searched the horizon for Rita but found no one following the team, not even at a distance. Maybe she was in the basket, injured or sick, he reasoned. But when he finally brought the team up even with his own, Mark could see that Rita was not with them.

"Where is she, Dandy?" Mark questioned, giving the dog

a rub on the muzzle. Dandy gave a yip as if trying to answer the question.

"I wish you could talk," Mark sighed. "I'd best feed you all instead and then we'll push on to find Rita."

❧

The delay cost Mark precious time, but he knew that the dogs had to be cared for. He piggybacked the sleds and harnessed Rita's dogs to run with his own. All the while Mark kept eyeing the skies and the ominous clouds that threatened his success.

When Mark finally put out once again to look for Rita, light was fading quickly. He scrutinized the trees for any sign that Rita might be nearby. There was nothing.

Mark was losing hope when flakes of snow began to fall. "God, please help me!" he called out. Just then Dandy yipped and followed it with a deep throaty howl. Mark halted the dogs and watched Dandy's actions. The dog strained in his harness and pulled to the right as if he planned to pull the entire team with him if necessary.

Mark turned the team and brought Dandy to the lead. "Take us to Rita, boy," he urged. "Find her for me."

Dandy began barking in urgency then. He knew what Mark expected of him and was more than willing to respond to the call. Mark moved the dogs out and allowed Dandy to choose the course. Within moments, Mark spotted something red in the distance. Rita had worn red coveralls. It had to be her.

When he got closer, Mark began to panic. She wasn't moving or acknowledging his calls. "Please God, don't let her die," Mark whispered.

Mark anchored the team and hurried forward to where Rita sat in a tight ball. She'd obviously tried to pack a wall of snow around her. "Rita!" he called and knelt down to push back her parka hood.

"Cold," Rita whimpered. "So cold."

Mark pulled her close and Rita moaned in agony. "Don't you go dying on me, Texas Rita." Mark tried to drawl good naturedly. "Otherwise, you'll never see Texas where the sun shines all the time and it's never cold."

Mark knew he was babbling, but his mind couldn't accept the possibility of Rita being anything other than healthy and strong. Hurrying back to the sled, Mark pulled out Rita's sleeping bag and his own as well. He brought both to where Rita had still not moved and began to work to get her wet parka off.

"Listen to me Rita," he said as he unzipped her coveralls. "I've got to get these wet things off of you. Hopefully, the clothes beneath your coveralls are dry. When we finish with this, I'll put you inside the sleeping bags. Do you understand?"

"I understand," Rita whispered.

Mark wasn't convinced. "What do you understand, Rita? Tell me what I said."

"You're going to put me in the sleeping bag," she said in an irritable tone, "and you didn't call me Texas Rita."

Mark grinned. She still had fight left in her. He wasn't too late!

"What about my dogs. I lost my team," Rita mumbled.

"Dandy found me," Mark answered. "They're safe and in good shape. I only hope we can say the same thing about you."

Mark knew that once he had Rita inside the bags, he'd have more time to set up a proper camp. He was one of those few racers who liked to have a tent along in case of an emergency, and this time, it served its purpose well. He put Dandy with Rita before going to work.

Camp was set up in record time. Mark soon had the tent up, with a hearty fire glowing in the cookstove. The time would have been even shorter had he not run back and forth to check on Rita.

"The tent's ready," Mark said as he lifted Rita in his arms. "I'm going to put you inside and then I'll get you something hot to drink."

Rita said nothing until Mark had deposited her inside the tent; then, with teeth chattering, she thanked him. "Mark, I don't know how you managed to find me, but I'm glad you did."

"Me, too," Mark said and reached out to touch Rita's frostbitten cheek. "You have no idea."

Then Mark went to get the hot coffee. When he returned with it, Rita wasn't sure she could even handle the cup. She felt as though her hands were on fire as they thawed and her mind still seemed blurred.

"Drink it down and I'll make you some soup. I've got packages of dried-chicken noodle," he said with a grin. "Isn't that suppose to be a cure-all?"

Rita smiled even though it hurt to do so. The skin on her face felt tight as though it might pull apart at the slightest movement. "I think it'll take more than chicken soup to cure what ails me."

Mark nodded. "I told you not to go out. I wish for once in your life you would have swallowed your pride and realized that sometimes others know best."

"I know I was wrong," Rita admitted. "I know it only too well."

"Well, this is a different side of you," Mark commented in surprise.

"Some people have to make their own foolish mistakes before they realize what fools they are. I guess I was one of those." Gone from Rita's voice was the severity and aloof reserve. "I just wanted to win the race. I wanted to show everyone that I could do it. . .that I didn't need anyone looking out for me."

"And now?" Mark questioned.

"Now, I know better," Rita replied. "I was scared to die, Mark. Not because I would never see Mom or Dad, or even you. . . ." She fell silent for a moment. "I didn't know what would happen. I didn't know where I would go or what death would really mean. I kept thinking about the Bible and the stories I'd learned as a child and a teenager. I thought of my mother's lectures on needing to be saved from my sins and I thought of what my father told me on the way to Anchorage."

"What was that?" Mark asked with a feeling he knew what Rita would say.

"Dad said, 'Rita, you must let go of the fear you feel inside.' He told me, 'Trust isn't an easy thing, but trust in God is something that will never let you down, because God will never let you down.' "

"Did you believe him?" Mark's face was stern, but his eyes were soft and warm.

"Not then," answered Rita.

"But what about now?"

"Now I realize I've been living on fear most all of my life. It's become such a part of my nature to distrust that I never saw the way it controlled me." Rita paused and looked thoughtfully at the cup in her hand before setting it aside.

"It's easy for other things to control us," Mark assured. "Things creep in that way and, before we realize it, we've become their victims. God's control isn't that way. He wants us to recognize Him as the controller. He wants us to see that He's in charge and find comfort in that fact."

Rita nodded. "I suppose I can see that now, but I've always been so independent." Outside, the wind picked up and moaned through the trees. "Even now, I'm skeptical. Not of God," she added at the look of bewilderment on Mark's face. "I'm skeptical that I can hand over the reins to my life and trust God to lead me."

"Do you want that, Rita?" Mark's question pierced Rita's heart.

From somewhere in Rita's memory, she began to quote Philippians Three, Verses Ten and Eleven. " 'That I may know him, and the power of his resurrection, and the fellowship of his sufferings, being made conformable unto his death; if by any means I might attain unto the resurrection of the dead.'"

"Truly, Rita? Do you want to accept Christ as your Savior?"

Rita hesitated only a moment. She didn't want to commit to God out of a sense of fear, yet wasn't she supposed to fear hell and eternal damnation? "I want to know about the love," she whispered with tears falling freely from her eyes. "I know about the fear and the pain of rejection, but I want to know about the love."

Mark's heart nearly broke for her. She was so vulnerable and childlike that he moved from his spot and put his arms around her. "God is love, Rita. I know you're familiar with that verse if you can quote Philippians."

Rita nodded and tried to wipe away her tears. "I think it's the first verse I memorized as a small girl."

"It's true," Mark continued. "God is love and He demonstrated His love for us in sending Christ to take our punishment. He doesn't want you to come only out of fear; after all, the Israelites feared Him long before He sent Christ to them. He wanted to draw His people to Him, to show them

His merciful love and eternal devotion. God loves His children, Rita. He loves you and He wants you to love Him."

"I do," Rita sobbed. "I always have, but my pride made me fear it. I just didn't want to get hurt again." She cried freely, unashamed of the tears.

Mark held her in silence until she was spent. When Rita finally lifted her face, her eyes were gentler than Mark had ever known them.

"Are you and God at peace now, Rita?"

"Yes," Rita replied. "I know Jesus says that He's the only way to come to God. I know the Bible well, I've just never lived by it. I've asked God to forgive me, Mark, but I don't believe for one minute that life will all of a sudden be wonderful and perfect. I've a great deal of my past to put right."

"What past?" Mark asked with a grin. "You're a new creation in Christ, right? You've sought forgiveness for all those sins and the Bible says God remembers them no more."

"Yes, but people aren't God and people remember them," Rita countered.

"People aren't responsible for your salvation, Rita." Mark drove his point home. "God is the one you answer to. God is the one who will clear the way for you to mend fences with others. Trust Him, Rita. He can handle the job."

Rita put her head upon Mark's shoulder, enjoying the comfort of another. "I know you're right, but I'm still afraid."

"There's a verse in Psalm Fifty-six just for you. It says, 'What time I am afraid, I will trust in Thee.' Trust doesn't come easy for you, Rita. I know that. But you can believe in this. You can trust God."

Rita remained silent, her dark eyes staring hopefully into Mark's. She basked in hope that Mark's encouragement would prove true. Trust was not an easy thing for Rita

Eriksson. But, trust in God was a start and Rita was eager to take that first wobbly step forward.

thirteen

The next day dawned bright and clear with frosty, cold temperatures that left a filigree of ice upon the tent walls. Rita found herself no worse for her experience and began the day by going outside and joining Mark in a hesitant prayer. After that, when the silence threatened to unnerve her, Rita fell back to her defensive nature.

"Shouldn't we be pushing on for Iditarod?" she questioned as she began to repack her sled.

"Definitely. We've lost a lot of time and since the weather has cleared, the others will no doubt have already passed us," Mark replied, acting as though it wasn't a big deal.

Rita's face fell. "I wanted to be the first to Iditarod. I wanted to give Dad the ingots."

"They wouldn't mean much to him," Mark replied. "He'd rather know that you enjoyed yourself and that you managed to stay alive and well."

"How would you know?" Rita retorted. "I know it meant a great deal to Dad to have won those ingots."

"Then you really don't know him very well at all," Mark spoke behind steamy breath.

"What's that suppose to mean. He is my father," Rita said emphasizing the word "my."

"The money, prizes, and laurels were never what drove your father to race the Iditarod," Mark began. "As a young man he traveled these trails in order to deliver the mail. He raced because he needed to prove to himself that he could do it one last time. He needed to taste the ice with each breath, to hear the silence of the interior, and feel the dogs working beneath his hands. The ingots never meant to him what they obviously mean to you."

Rita felt a rage building inside her. How dare Mark tell her what her father felt, or who he was. She opened her mouth to speak and then shut it again. What could she say that would make any sense? It wasn't easy to refute the truth. Mark was right and that's what bothered her most. She walked away to consider his words, still feeling his eyes burning holes through her façade.

⁂

Retracing their way back to the trail proved easier than either one had imagined. Rita was surprised to learned that she'd been only a matter of miles from Iditarod. Somehow, through the blizzard and all of the trials that had plagued her way, Rita had still managed to keep the team going in the right direction.

"That's some nose," Mark teased as they made their way to the checkpoint officials. "You wandered around, blind in a snow storm for three days, and still managed to put yourself in a decent position to regain the lost time."

Rita said nothing as people pressed in around her.

"We'd just about given up hope of finding you," one man remarked behind a fur-trimmed parka. "Are you injured?"

"No," Rita answered. "A little frostbite on my face, but nothing serious."

"I guess that's pretty typical," the man laughed. "I've heard more than one racer talk about his or her new Iditarod skin. Losing frostbitten skin off your face is pretty routine and the skin beneath is baby soft."

Rita smiled and waited for the officials to check her dogs over. She'd lost track of Mark and it wasn't until she overheard a comment by the man who'd first spoken to her that Rita realized something was wrong.

"I'm sorry," she said, placing a hand on the man's parka, "I couldn't help overhear your comment that Mark Williams is in some kind of trouble."

The man turned and pushed back his parka enough to reveal a weather-lined face with a graying beard. "He disqualified himself coming out after you. He disobeyed the official's direct order to stay in Ophir after a freeze was put on the race."

"But he only left to come after me. What about the Good Samaritan Rule? It wasn't that he was trying to get ahead in the race. No doubt there are plenty of racers who've moved out ahead of us. Mark isn't a threat to anyone's victory," Rita protested.

"I'm just working here," the man said and threw up his hands. "But as I understand it, the problem isn't that he helped you so much as he disregarded a direct order. The real decision has to come from a three-member panel of the race officials. They're appointed by the Iditarod Race Marshall and they have to reach a unanimous decision."

"Then I need to get word to them," Rita said, suddenly fearing that Mark would have come all this way, only to be disqualified by an unselfish act of concern for her.

"I'm not sure what to tell you," the man replied. "You'd probably better talk to the man in charge. He's over there in the blue coveralls."

"Thank you." Rita saw to her dogs, then went in search of the race official.

და

Although Rita had fully intended to push right out of Iditarod and head for Shageluk on the Innoko River, she found herself unable to continue until she learned of Mark's fate.

She'd explained everything she could to the official and pleaded Mark's case in every way she could conceive. The man had been sympathetic and considerate of her testimony and promised that the officials would take everything into consideration. The answer would be radioed to them within a matter of minutes.

"I'm sorry for the trouble I've caused you, Mark." Rita's sincerity was evident as she took a seat beside her father's partner.

"I would do it all again," Mark said in a peaceful way that eluded Rita.

"Aren't you angry?"

"No," Mark said with a shake of his head. "Why should I be?" He looked up from where he'd been mending a harness. Mark was never one for wasting a single minute. "Anger wouldn't change a thing and would only ruin this beautiful day."

"I've possibly cost you the race. They may not let you finish the Iditarod. Doesn't that mean anything? After all, that's why we're here," Rita argued.

"I would debate that," Mark said matter-of-factly. "God has many purposes for us in life. I believe it's entirely possible that the only reason I raced this year was in order to be there for you. God knew you'd need help, both physically and spiritually. If He used me for that purpose, then I'm content."

"You mean to tell me," Rita began, "that you wouldn't be the least bit disappointed if they disqualified you here and now?"

"Of course I'd be disappointed," Mark replied. "I planned for this race all year, just like you did. I'm just saying that the race isn't everything. I made the decision, knowing full well what the possible consequences could be. You nearly lost your life out there, Rita. Is life so unimportant to you that you wouldn't risk being disqualified from the Iditarod if it meant that you could save someone from dying?"

Rita swallowed hard. She'd always put herself first and now she couldn't honestly say whether she would have given up her lead, even the race, to help someone else out of their own foolishness. Suddenly, Rita felt repulsed at the image she had of herself. Would she really have let someone die?

Mark sensed the inner struggle in Rita. His sympathy for her was evident. "You've had a hard time of it, Rita. Nevertheless, I don't doubt for one minute that you would not only risk disqualification of the race, but that you'd risk your very life in order to save another. You aren't the vicious, heartless person you believe yourself to be."

"I don't know about that," Rita admitted. "You may know my father well, but you don't know me."

Mark smiled in a way that caused Rita's heart to race. "I think I know you better than you imagine."

"Just because you rescued me, doesn't mean you know everything about me." Rita's words were strangely soft spoken.

"I wouldn't pretend to know everything about you, Miss Eriksson," Mark said with a chuckle. "I just propose to have more insight than you give me credit for."

"Williams!" the race official's voice rang out. He crossed the distance with long, quick strides. "The panel has cleared you to continue. You haven't been disqualified!"

The small crowd that had waited to hear the announcement gave up a cheer, while Mark and Rita embraced without thinking.

"I'm so glad!" Rita nearly squealed. Mark wrapped his arms around her, lifting her into the air and twirling her around.

"Me, too!" he replied then placed a kiss firmly upon Rita's lips.

Rita found herself returning Mark's kiss before her mind could offer up any protest. She lingered in his arms while the people around them offered congratulatory praises and encouraging words. When the revelry died down, Rita's senses seemed to return. She became very aware of Mark's firm hold and dropped her arms.

Raising her eyes slowly, she found Mark's laughing eyes and smug expression. "I told you I knew you better than you think."

Rita felt her face turn hot in spite of the subzero temperatures. She pushed away from Mark, stammering for something to say, but words escaped her.

"You'd best get a move on it," someone said and Rita nodded.

"Yes, I'm going," she said and backed away from Mark. He was still standing there, looking quite satisfied with himself, when Rita finished securing her team.

❧

Mushing out of Iditarod, Rita's mind moved in a hundred different directions. She'd become a Christian, but what did that really mean in the way that she'd now live her life? Could she somehow find a way to reach out to her mother and overcome the past?

She smiled to herself as she imagined her father's pleasure in her decision to accept Christ. He could rest easy now and that gave Rita peace. Maybe it wasn't too late to make up for the past.

She tried to ignore the images of Mark in her mind, but when his voice called out behind her in the traditional, "Trail!" requesting that she yield the right-of-way to his passing team, Rita couldn't help but think of him.

She glanced up behind dark glasses as Mark gave her a brief salute and was gone. Watching his team disappear in the distance, Rita found that she had no desire to pursue him. She needed distance between them. Distance to think and to understand why she'd so shamelessly reacted to Mark's kiss.

≈

After eight days on the Iditarod, the Yukon River presented itself to Rita. She was tired of the ice, cold, and wind, but that was what this race was all about—that and inner strength, guts and sheer willpower.

Now over six hundred fifty miles from the starting line of the race with a little over five hundred yet to go, sleep was quickly becoming a thing of the past.

Rita found the breaks shorter in length and farther apart. She craved sleep like a starving man craved food. Pushing north on the frozen river, Rita found it necessary to strap herself to the sled to prevent falling off of it when she dozed. She struggled to stay awake, hearing voices that weren't there, seeing sights that had never known creation in the real world.

She made her checkpoints at Grayling, Eagle Island, and finally Kaltag before moving west toward the Bering Sea and Unalakleet. Following trails that were centuries old, Rita pressed her team along the Kaltag Portage for nearly one hundred miles. The routine of fighting fierce winds and death defying cold with brief naps and feeding periods took an even greater toll. Rita was nearing exhaustion and wouldn't feel free to sleep for any long period of time until she reached White Mountain where she'd have to take a mandatory six-hour stopover. Until then she'd have to catch just bits and pieces of rest on the way.

Unalakleet, "place where the east wind blows," was an

Inupiat Eskimo village of nearly eight hundred people. Positioned on the Bering Sea, this small town represented the place where camaraderie gave way to competition. It was here that racers would dump off all but their most necessary equipment and often pick up sleek, lightweight racing sleds for the final push into Nome.

After a welcome of sirens and bells from the town's natives, Rita fed the dogs and left them to rest while she changed over her sled and made decisions about her supplies. Every time a new team came into sight, the revelry would sound again, reminding Rita of her competition. In all the time since she'd last seen Mark, Rita hadn't even thought to check on his progress. Now Rita's only competition was herself. It wasn't that she didn't want to win the race, it was just that everything had changed on the way to Iditarod. Now, it was enough to push herself to the limit and do her best without causing harm to the team or risking them in any way.

Each team was appointed to a Unalakleet family and cared for during their stopover. Rita was grateful for her host family and made her way to an offered meal and bed, after finishing with her sled. It was a tradition Rita totally approved of and found herself thanking God for as she set her alarm and fell instantly into deep sleep.

❧

Hours later, Rita awoke to a rosy dawn and steaming coffee. She ate and chatted with her host before seeing to her duties. With the final stretches of the race ahead of her, Rita would do as most of the other team drivers did and reduce the number of dogs on her team. She had mentally calculated each choice after watching her dogs on the trail.

She walked quickly among the dogs, surveying and deciding before finally reducing the team to ten. The other dogs were then taken to the holding pens to be flown back to Anchorage. It was hard to part with any of them and Rita felt almost as though she were betraying them, even knowing that it was for their benefit.

Reluctantly, Rita departed Unalakleet following two other teams as the trail rose into the coastal Blueberry Hills. Their next checkpoint would be Shaktoolik.

Rita found herself surprisingly invigorated after her rest in Unalakleet. Maybe it was changing the sled and dropping the dogs, but whatever it was, Rita suddenly found herself revitalized and eager to race.

She pushed out against the twenty mile-an-hour gusts that bore down from the northwest, to pass two teams. With each gained position she felt the race spirit alive and well within her heart. She wanted to do well and make her father proud!

Shaktoolik was only forty miles from Unalakleet and the time passed so quickly that Rita could scarcely believe her good fortune. She had gained a total of three positions and learned that another four teams ahead of her were still resting at the checkpoint. Deciding to push on, Rita's enthusiasm was picked up by the dogs who yipped and strained to be down the trail at a run.

Land soon gave way to frozen Norton Bay. This was the part of the race that Rita had feared most. It unnerved her to realize as her team moved out across the ice, that beneath her was nothing but water. Sure, there was a thick frozen surface, but an early warming or sudden storm could quickly create a life and death situation.

The skies were still clear, however, and in spite of the strong winds, Rita found the trail markers easily. She settled her nerves by reminding herself that all was in God's hands and pulled her parka hood tight against the wind.

She stopped once on the icy surface to change booties on her dogs and offer them a quick snack of honeyballs. Her fingers numbed as she whipped off her gloves and mittens to pull off worn, tattered booties and replace them with new ones.

Soon they were back on their way and Rita looked forward to the next checkpoint. For the first time she found herself wanting to know what Mark's ranking was and how he was doing. With a fondness that startled her, she remembered his embrace. She wanted to let go of her fears and reach out to Mark, but should she?

"What should I do, God?" Rita found herself praying. "For so many years I've put people away from me. I've fought to keep my distance and never let people too close. I can't ignore how Mark made me feel, Lord, but what do I do?"

Conditions started to deteriorate as Rita's team approached the checkpoint at Koyuk on the opposite shore of Norton Bay. The winds had picked up to a fierce forty miles per hour, with a heavy blizzard to present near whiteout conditions. Rita pulled into the checkpoint riding on sheer nerves and adrenaline.

"You're doing a fine job, Ms. Eriksson," the official told her. "How are you dogs doing?"

"Great," Rita gasped for air; she had run the last mile to lighten the load for her dogs.

"You've moved into nineteenth place," the man added as he walked away.

"Wait a minute," Rita called out. "What about Mark Williams?"

"Let me see," the man replied and paused to check his list. "He was here eight hours ago.

Rita smiled to herself. "Thanks. Has anyone crossed the

finish line yet?

"Not yet, but it's getting close. Several of the front run-ners will soon be within reach of it. My guess on a finish time will be thirteen days and some odd hours."

"Fantastic!" Rita exclaimed. She couldn't imagine the speed that the others would have to maintain to pull off a thirteen-day race completion. Her own pace had been gru-eling enough.

"Let him do well, Lord," Rita whispered as she went about heating food and water for the dogs. "I want Mark to do well," she added, knowing that she meant it with all her heart.

fourteen

Rita crossed the finish line in Nome, amidst the cheers of well-wishers and residents. Television cameras still worked to capture the race; the healthy finish of Rita in seventeenth place position merited special attention. It would also earn her the sum of six thousand dollars. Rita found herself calculating expenses for the race; they might just break even.

Rita answered questions for the press, giving them her outlook and feel for the final miles of the trail. They also quizzed her about her lost days near Iditarod and Rita was quick to give Mark credit for her rescue.

"I probably wouldn't be here now, if it weren't for Mark Williams," Rita told a newspaper reporter. "He risked not only disqualification from the race, but his life in order to go out and search for me."

"Mark Williams is your father's partner in the Eriksson Dog Kennel, is he not?" the man questioned her.

"That's true," Rita admitted. "He's also a good friend of the family."

"Any chance that you and he are more than good friends?" the man asked with a grin.

Rita was surprised at the question and noticed that the other reporters awaited her answer with an almost anxious look.

"I'd say that's between Rita and me," Mark's voice rang out from somewhere behind the crowd. "Now, if you don't mind, we need to care for the dogs." Then in a whisper for only Rita's ears, Mark added, "Good to see you, Texas Rita."

There was a bustle of activity and several other questions posed, but Mark waved them off and managed to pull Rita away from the press.

"Why did you bait them like that?" Rita asked, forgetting how happy she was to see him.

Mark laughed. "I thought it sounded good." Mark thrust his gloved hands deep into his pockets and shrugged his shoulders. Rita thought he looked rather like a little boy who'd been caught red-handed with the cookie jar.

"But you saw the way they reacted to your reply. You might as well have told them something far-fetched, like we were planning our wedding," retorted Rita.

Mark grinned and reached out to take hold of her arm. "And what would be so bad about that?"

Rita stared up in shocked surprise. She opened her mouth to answer but never got the chance for just then her Aunt Julie appeared in the path before them.

"Aunt Julie!" Rita cried and fell into the older woman's arms. "I'm so glad you're here. I wasn't sure I'd make it, but I knew you'd be waiting here for me and that helped me to push on."

"I knew you could do it," Julie remarked beneath layers of mufflers and fur. "You've got that tenacious Swedish blood from your Grandfather Eriksson. You put your mind to complete the race and the rest just followed naturally."

Rita laughed at her aunt's words. She turned to say something to Mark, only to realize he'd slipped away from her. She looked around her, hoping to catch a glimpse of him, but to no avail. People filled in every inch of the street and the noise was incredible.

"Are you looking for that young man of yours?" Julie

questioned loudly.

Rita put her hands on her hips and with a raised eyebrow asked, "Why do you call him, 'that young man of yours?' "

Julie smile. "Never mind. We can talk about it at home. I've got a bed ready and waiting."

"A real bed?" Rita teasingly questioned. She looked among the crowd for her Uncle Sam before turning back to Julie. "Where's Uncle Sam? I can't imagine that he'd miss the race. He isn't sick, is he?"

Julie patted Rita's arm. "You worry too much. I said we'd catch everything up at home. Come on." Julie motioned to Rita but she held back.

"Really, it sounds great," Rita sighed, "But first—"

"First come the dogs," Julie interrupted and laughed. "They always come first," she added, linking her arm with Rita's. "Oh, by the way," Julie said with a wink, "Mark came in fifth."

❧

Rita's dogs were taken in crates to the airport, but not before she gave each one a heartfelt thank you. Dandy seemed to sense that he'd done quite well and jumped up and down in his harness, until Rita finally calmed him down. She stood watching the transport truck disappear down the road when she felt familiar hands on her shoulders.

"Hi, Seventeen," Mark's deep voice called out in the silence.

Rita turned quickly, at least calling her seventeen wouldn't require an explanation. "Mark! I wondered where you went. Thanks for the help with the dogs. I still can't believe I really finished the race."

"No problem," Mark replied, acting as though their earlier conversation had never taken place. "I did want to point out however, you weren't there to greet me as I crossed the finish line." His teasing nature was infectious.

Rita couldn't help but grin. "I know, Number Five. I guess next year I'll just have to rectify that problem."

"Next year?" Mark questioned with a chuckle. "What makes you think I'll let you come next year?"

"What makes you presume that you'll have any say?" Rita's determined look made Mark back down with a laugh.

"I guess we can discuss it later," he added.

"Everyone keeps saying that," Rita replied and picked up the bag of things she'd decided to keep with her rather than ship back home. "I'm staying with my aunt, Julie Curtiss. I'm sure you'd be welcome to drop over."

"Maybe I will," Mark answered. "We'll see."

❧

Rita followed her Aunt Julie up the long shoveled walkway, grateful that she'd finally be able to take a hot shower and sleep in a real bed.

Julie unlocked the door of her two-storied house and ushered her niece inside; the pungent aroma of flowers filled the air.

"Umm," Rita said, putting her bag down on the entryway floor. "It smells like a florist shop in here."

"It should," Julie replied and led Rita to the living room where flowers and potted plants graced every table top.

"They're beautiful!" Rita exclaimed. "Where did they all come from?"

"Sam's funeral," Julie said softly. "He died the day you started the Iditarod."

Rita dropped quietly into a nearby chair. "Dead? Uncle Sam is dead?"

Julie pulled off her heavy coat and cast it aside. "Yes. I

know it's hard to believe. I wish there could have been an easier way to tell you." Julie couldn't help but sympathize with the great shock her niece had just been dealt. August hadn't handled it any better when Julie had telephoned him with the news.

"It's hard for me to accept, because it feels as though he's right here. His things are still here. His guitar still sits in its case against the wall. His reading glasses are still on the table over there," Julie said and pointed.

"Wha. . .what happened?" Rita asked as tears spilled down her cheeks.

"He died in his sleep, Rita." Julie smiled. "We'd had a wonderful evening with friends and had come home to discuss you and the race. Sam bet you'd place in the top twenty and sure enough, here you are. Then we climbed into bed, talked some more, and held each other close. When I woke up in the morning he was gone."

"You talk about it so calmly," Rita sobbed. "I don't know how you bear it."

"Sam's not all that far away," Julie answered. "He's not gone forever. . .he's just waiting in Heaven."

Rita nodded. "But you're here, Aunt Julie."

Julie smiled and eased back against the chair. "Yes, that is the hard part. I must wait and join him later. But you know, a long time ago when I traveled the old village trails as a public health nurse, Sam often had to wait for me here at home.

"I remember how hard the separation was and how eagerly I would hurry home to be with him again. Sam always kept a light burning for me in the window. . .it was our way of letting the other one know that we'd not forgotten them." Julie got up and crossed the room. She pulled back heavy drapery to reveal a small lamp. It's soft glowing bulb burned as a bright reminder that Sam was not forgotten.

"I know that Sam's burning one for me in Heaven," Julie said, with a single tear touching her wrinkled cheek. "I'll make my way home when the time is right."

Rita rushed to her aunt and held her. "Oh, Aunt Julie, I'm so sorry he's gone. I loved him a great deal. He always made me laugh," her voice broke into sobs. "I'm sorry that I'm not offering you comfort. . .blubbering as I am."

"It's all right, Rita. I miss him, too. I didn't say it was easy. But at least I know where he is."

Rita nodded and pulled back and wiped her eyes. "Aunt Julie, I asked Jesus to be my Savior." The sudden revelation seemed fitting.

Julie's face lit up with such joy that Rita thought she would shout. "I've prayed that you would. Now, you don't have to worry about death. Not Sam's or mine, or even your mom or dad's. You'll see us again in Heaven and you don't need to fear life or death."

Rita shook her head. "I want it to be that real to me, Aunt Julie, but. . . ."

"But?"

Rita led Julie to the sofa where both women dropped wearily.

"But, I don't feel anything really different. Oh, I think I feel peace. You know, the kind of peace that you get when you stop fighting something and give in. You're still not sure you understand what you're getting yourself into, but you feel better in just having done something."

Julie laughed. "Oh, Rita, I do understand. Let me assure you, God is very much alive and working in your heart. Your salvation is quite real."

Rita shook her head. "I want to believe that. I said the

words and I believed them true. It's just that I don't know what comes next. Doesn't that sound stupid? I mean, here I am, a church kid who spent a lifetime involved in Sunday school and Bible memory contests, but I don't know what to do next or how to find out."

Julie took Rita's hand in her own aged one. "Rita, God loves you. You understand this, don't you?"

"Of course," Rita replied.

"No, I mean," Julie reemphasized the words. "God loves you, Rita. God loves Rita Eriksson."

Rita's puzzled look caused Julie to continue. "God knows you better than you know yourself, Rita. He formed you in your mother's womb and molded you into the person you became. He patiently waited for you to turn back to Him and, because He loved you, Rita, He gave you a way back through Jesus. You can count on that way to be real, and even when though you can't see the bridge that Jesus' sacrifice gave you, it's there.

"It's that old issue of trust," Julie continued. "God has given many promises in the Bible. You don't have to worry that some are true and others aren't. God didn't allow the Word to be created for some kind of show. It's genuine and real and it offers you all the guidance and hope that you will ever need. You must have the faith to accept God's gift and live for Him."

Rita nodded slowly. "I guess my faith is very weak."

"No, Rita," Julie said, squeezing Rita's hand. "It's just newborn. It's tiny and small, but very much alive and surprisingly strong. Give it time and it will grow as you feed on the Word and rest in the Lord. Now," Julie said as she glanced at the clock on her wall, "catching up on everything else will wait. You need to go to bed. Come along."

Julie showed Rita to her room and gave her a kiss on the cheek before closing the door. Rita shed her coveralls and dropped to her knees. "Oh, God, thank You for Aunt Julie. She's such a strong and wise woman. I want to know You like she does and I want my faith to grow." Rita started to get to her feet, but stopped. "And, Lord, please help her not to be lonely without Uncle Sam, Amen."

fifteen

The next day Rita answered the door of her Aunt Julie's house while her aunt prepared breakfast in the kitchen.

A young man stood holding a white box and clipboard. "I have a delivery for Rita Eriksson," he said as he studied the paper.

"That's me," Rita replied and signed for the delivery. She tipped the delivery man and went back to the warmth of her aunt's kitchen.

"Just what we need," Rita mused, "more flowers."

"Who are they from?" Julie questioned as she loaded the table with more food than she or Rita could possibly finish.

"I don't know," Rita replied and opened the large box. Inside was a stately looking, white, Stetson hat. "Well, what do you know," Rita gasped, staring at the hat.

Julie peered over her shoulder. "We've better use for that than flowers. Who's it from?"

Rita couldn't speak for a moment. She new full well who the hat was from, but it would be impossible to explain to Julie. "Here's the card," Rita finally replied. "It says, 'Congratulations, Texas Rita. What's so far-fetched about—' " Rita fell silent as she glanced over the words that followed.

"What's so far-fetched about what?" Julie inquired, joining Rita at the table. "And what's with the Texas Rita stuff?"

Rita shook her head. The gift was from Mark and he wanted to know what was so far-fetched about their planning a wedding. How could Rita explain that to her aunt?

"It's nothing, Julie," she said and put the card in her

141

pocket. "It's from Mark and he's just giving me a hard time because I once mentioned wanting to move to Texas."

"He's a good man, Rita." Julie's words were true and Rita knew it full well.

"I know," she finally murmured and waited for Julie to pray over their food.

Julie sensed Rita's apprehension to discuss the matter anymore. Instead, she prayed a short blessing and offered her niece breakfast.

Rita felt relief to see that Julie was willing to drop the matter. Now, if only she could avoid Mark. There was no way she'd be able to face him and discuss anything rationally.

There were several parties and presentations at which Rita would have to be present. Of course, she could always feign being sick, but that would go against her new-found principles. Besides, it would no doubt bring Mark to her side, and in the privacy of her aunt's home, Rita knew it would be more than she could bear.

Rita made plans for her trip back to Anchorage amidst meeting her obligations in finishing the formalities of the race. There was a party she was to attend that would honor all those who'd run the race. Julie had agreed to accompany Rita, but on the night of the party, Julie was sick in bed with a bad cold.

"I'll be just fine, Rita," Julie chided her niece. "You go to the party and have fun. I'm just being cautious with myself, knowing how easily I seem to contract pneumonia."

"But I could stay here and take care of you," Rita said, nearly pleading. She was desperate to stay out of Mark's reach.

"I wouldn't hear of it. You've earned your laurels. I insist you go and party with your friends and have a good time. I'm sure if you called Mark at the hotel, he'd be more than happy to come escort you to the party," Julie added.

"Yes, I'm sure he would be," Rita said and walked to the door. "That's what I'm afraid of."

Julie chuckled and covered it with a cough. Rita knew her aunt was good naturedly trying to help her to see the good side of Mark's interest. Rita just shook her head, however, and went to get ready for the party.

❧

The evening passed without mishap and Rita was beginning to have confidence that she just might avoid Mark, when suddenly he was at her side.

"I'd like to have a moment of your time," he whispered in her ear. Taking hold of her hand, he added, "If you aren't too busy."

Rita trembled at his touch and her eyes darkened to ebony. Against her will, she looked up and saw the determination in Mark's face.

"All right." She barely got the words out before Mark was leading her down the corridor to the coat-check room.

"Let's walk," he suggested and called for their coats.

Rita felt her stomach turn flip-flops when Mark helped her on with her coat. She heard an inner voice that told her to run back to the safety of her aunt's house, but her legs refused to move.

"Are you ready?" Mark questioned, seeing that Rita was rooted in place. "You ought to have a good hat," he added with a grin.

It pulled Rita from her stupor. "I have one," she said with a smirk, "but my boots don't match."

Mark laughed heartily. "We'll have to rectify that."

❧

Outside, the town was still overrun with visitors and extended race parties. Mark lead Rita down a quiet side street and off to a more secluded part of town. Rita sensed Mark growing more serious.

"I've wanted to talk to you for days, but you were avoiding me," Mark began. "I figured out if I didn't force my hand I'd have to wait until we got back to your folks' house and I didn't want to wait."

Rita didn't even look up. She shuffled along at Mark's side waiting for the rest of his speech.

"I don't know why you are having trouble facing me, Rita." Mark's words weren't what Rita had expected.

Her head snapped up and the independent spirit in her won over. "I'm not having trouble facing you," she lied.

"You sure you want to stay with that story, ma'am?" Mark questioned, sounding every bit the law official.

"No, I. . .well. . .," Rita stammered. "So I was avoiding you. What of it?"

Mark laughed out loud and pulled Rita with him. "Come on, let's have some coffee. I know a quiet little place."

Rita soon found herself seated with Mark, as the only guests of the small cafe. Mark ordered them coffee and continued his conversation as though nothing had caused any break in his thought.

"Why are you avoiding me, Rita?"

"I don't know," she managed to answer. Her cheeks were flushed and her stomach churned. Why couldn't he just drop the subject and talk about something else.

"I think you do know," Mark pressed. "I think you know how I feel about you and I think you feel the same way."

"I don't know what you're talking about," Rita replied, and turned her attention to the coffee that the waitress had just brought.

"I've come to care a great deal about you, Rita. At first, I thought it was just because of my loyalty to August, but that passed real quick," he said with a grin. "I love you, Rita."

The words were bold and without hesitation, no teasing and not a hint of sarcasm. Rita nearly spit out her coffee at the declaration. Her eyes opened wide and her mouth dropped open. How could he say something so important with no more warning than that?

"You what?" She thought she'd only questioned Mark in her mind, but the words vocalized themselves aloud.

"You heard me," Mark replied patiently. "I love you. Furthermore, I want you to be my wife. I want us to get married right away, even before we go back home."

"I don't believe this," Rita gasped. "I can't believe that you're saying any of this."

"Would you like me to get down on one knee?" he teased.

"I'm serious," Rita said in an offended tone. "How can you joke at a time like this?"

"I'm serious," Mark said, moving from the chair to put one knee on the floor.

"Get up," Rita said between clenched teeth. "Get up before somebody sees you."

"I won't get up until you say that you'll marry me," Mark restated.

Rita wanted to run, but instead tears came to her eyes and before she could control them, she was nearly hysterical. Mark got up and quickly offered her his handkerchief.

"I'm sorry, Rita," he said softly. He sat back down and waited for Rita to regain control of her emotions.

"No," Rita whispered. "I'm the one who's sorry. You're a good man and I can't imagine why you would continue to care about me after all that's taken place between us."

"The past is gone," Mark offered. "I don't hold anything

against you and I hope you don't hold anything against me."

"I don't," Rita said, shaking her head. "I just can't deal with all of this right now. I don't know what I feel or think. I was just trying to understand Christianity and where I stood with God and now this. I can't do it, Mark. I can't deal with you and God at the same time."

"But you've resolved your relationship with God. I was there, remember? I know that you've got a lot of questions, but they'll all get answers in time." Mark paused for a moment still feeling disbelief for Rita's display of emotions. "I know you care about me. No, I'm certain you love me," Mark proclaimed.

Rita dried her eyes and held back the torrent of new tears that threatened to flow. "I'm glad you're certain, because I don't know what I feel."

They sat in silence for several minutes before Mark surprised them both and got to his feet. "I do love you, Rita. There will always be a place for you back home. I'll be there and you'll know where to find me. Just remember this," he added with a gentle smile, "I'm not the kind of man who gives up. I'm very patient and I can wait you out. Some day you'll come to me and I'll be there with open arms just for you, Texas Rita."

He threw some money down on the table and walked from the cafe, still carrying his coat. Rita stared after him in wonderment. He wasn't mad or if he was, he held it in so that not a single trace made itself known to Rita.

She marveled at his confidence and peace. "How could he be so certain of his feelings?" she whispered. Yet, even as she questioned his actions, Rita knew in her heart that he was right. She did care for him. She did love him. But how was she supposed to deal with those feelings?

Rita left the cafe and took the long way back to her aunt's

house. She had to think things through and, in spite of the cold, Rita took her time pondering the situation.

"Aunt Julie was right," Rita muttered aloud. "I'm afraid to trust Mark, just like I was afraid to trust God." She fell silent and wondered if perhaps she was still afraid to trust God.

"It's all so new to me, God," she whispered to the night air. "I know that I'm supposed to have faith and to trust, but you know that doesn't come easy for me. Now, Mark is asking for the same thing. He wants to marry me, Lord. What am I supposed to do?"

She approached the Curtiss house and caught sight of the light in the window—Sam's light, Julie's light. The reminder of a love that had lasted through childbirth, death, wars, and all that came from the process of living.

Rita thought of the way Sam would look at Julie. There had always been so much love in his eyes and Rita had marveled at it even as a teenager. How could anyone ever share a love like that and make it last a lifetime?

Rita looked up to the skies as if hoping that some celestial answer would be written across the heavens. Could it be possible that Mark loved her in the same way that Sam had loved Julie? Was it possible that Rita was throwing away her only chance for that kind of love?

She made her way quickly into the house and nearly ran up the stairs to get to her aunt's room. A light from beneath the door gave Rita all the prompting she needed.

She knocked lightly and called, "Aunt Julie, are you still awake?"

"Come on in, Rita," Julie answered. "What's going on?"

Rita left her coat in the hall and crossed the room to her aunt's bed. "I need to talk."

Julie smiled and patted the bed. "Have a seat and tell me

what's on your mind."

Rita lost no time. "Mark asked me to marry him."

Julie clapped her hands together. "How wonderful!"

Rita frowned. "I told him no."

"You did what?" Julie questioned.

"I told him no. Oh, Aunt Julie, I can't marry Mark. I don't know how I feel about him. One minute I think I love him, the next minute I don't think I even know the meaning of the word." Rita threw up her hands. "How can I promise to love and cherish someone, when I'm not even sure what it means to love."

"But, Rita," said Julie, "you've known what it is to be loved and to love. You've had your family and friends—"

"No," Rita interrupted. "I never felt loved by any of my friends. I always kept them at arm's length. It was my fault, but, Aunt Julie, I never let any of them get close enough to love them or for them to love me."

"But your family," Julie protested, "they love you and surely you love them. You love me, don't you?"

"Of course," Rita replied. It hurt so much to think her aunt might question her love. "You've always been there for me. You've always loved me."

"Well then, what is it?" Julie continued. "Your mother and father love you. Your brothers and sisters love you. How can you say you don't know how to love or be loved?"

Rita hung her head. "I hardly know my brothers and sisters."

"Whose fault is that?" Julie questioned sternly.

"I know it's partially my fault," Rita admitted. "But some of it is their fault."

"You can't deal with other than what you, yourself, control. Your anger and alienation toward them is where you must begin. Let go of the past and the distances that separated you. When you get home, why not write each of them a long letter. Tell them how you feel. I think you'd be surprised at their response," Julie suggested.

"What about Mother?" Rita finally braved the question.

"What about her?"

"She never wanted me, Aunt Julie. I heard her say it. She can't love me, if she didn't even want me." Rita broke down.

"Talk to her, Rita. Talk to her and let her explain. I know Beth loves you and I know it hurts her when she believes, by your actions, that you don't love her," Julie said, holding her arms open to Rita's sobbing form.

Rita fell into her aunt's embrace like a small, hurt child. "I want her to love me, Aunt Julie. I want my mother to love me."

"Child, she already does. Give her a chance to show you," Julie said in a calming way. "Give them all a chance, Rita. Your mother, God, Mark. . .let them show you how important you are to them. Let them love you."

sixteen

Anchorage looked almost foreign to Rita. She realized how little attention she'd paid the town before the race. After living there for five years, she'd taken it for granted. Now, looking out from her hotel window, Rita found herself wishing she could be back in Tok.

For over an hour she watched as the townspeople hustled to beat the clock. Traffic moved at a quick clip along the busy, inner-city streets, while pedestrians fought competitively for their right to cross intersections.

Store windows sported huge signs that called the public inside to late winter sales and discounted prices. It was all so busy, so noisy, and completely out of sync with what Rita had just spent doing for the last year.

Rita was surprised to find that she missed the quiet of her woods and the vast openness of rural life. She missed the dogs and the roar of the wind through the trees. Even the northern lights would be difficult to see through the harsh city lights. Rita longed for home.

"What am I going to do now?" she whispered to the city. "I don't belong here and I want to go home. But should I go back?"

And what of Mark? her heart questioned. He loved her and she knew she loved him. Dare she give up her independence and tear down the walls that separated them? Dare she return his love as openly as he gave his?

A knock at the door brought Rita back to reality. She crossed the room, opened the door, and found her parents on the other side.

"Mom! Dad!" squealed Rita. She embraced them both at once and missed the look of surprise they shared over her shoulder. "I wondered when you were going to get here. How are you? How are the dogs?"

"Fine to both questions," August said with a laugh. "If I didn't know better, I'd say you missed us."

"What makes you think you know better?" Rita questioned. "I did miss you and I'm very glad to see you here. In fact, I have something important to tell you both."

August and Beth steadied each other. With Rita it was hard to tell what she might have in mind. Over the years they'd learned to take her declarations in stride and knew better than to try and anticipate what their daughter might say.

"Come and sit down," Rita said, taking them to a small table. "There are only two chairs, so I'll sit on the bed."

Her parents nodded and moved almost apprehensively to the chairs. Rita swallowed hard and tried to think of just the right words.

"I did a lot of thinking out on the trail," she began. "I know the reports of my foolishness have already reached the papers and television, so I realize how worried you must have been. I want to apologize for not calling you, but I had to think through a great deal."

August and Beth hung on their daughter's every word. They had worried about her. Worried that her stubborn pride would claim her life and remembered having to sit by and wait until news of their youngest confirmed that she was safe.

Rita paused for a moment. She still had a touch of pride that worried about her mother's reaction to her declaration of faith. If Beth reacted smugly, Rita just knew she'd run from the room. Steadying her nerves, Rita continued.

"Mark found me when I'd just about given up hope of going on. I'd lost the team and things looked pretty bad. I'd managed to make a windbreak by packing snow, but I knew I couldn't last long without my gear and the dogs. Then Mark showed up and everything turned around. That night we talked a lot and I came to be sorry for the problems my stubbornness and independence have caused."

"What are you trying to say, Rita?" August asked.

Rita drew a deep breath. "I guess I'm trying to apologize for the way I've acted in the past. I gave up my pride and accepted Christ as my Savior." She waited and watched Beth for the reaction she feared, but the only thing she saw were the tears in her mother's eyes.

August nodded. "That must have been the hardest decision you've ever made."

Rita was amazed at the peace that settled over the room. She had been so sure of how her parents would respond that she'd literally spent hours deciding how she, herself, would react.

"It was," Rita finally replied.

Beth wiped away the tears in her eyes, but remained silent. Rita thought there was a gentler look to her mother. Was it Rita's decision to accept Christ that made her so? Or was Rita just truly seeing her mother for the first time?

A knock sounded at the door and Rita hesitantly answered it. There was still much more she wanted to say, especially to her mother. She didn't like the idea of an interruption.

"Yes?" she questioned the hotel employee who waited on the other side.

"Is Mr. Eriksson here?"

"Yes, I'm August Eriksson," August said, coming to stand beside Rita.

"There's a gentleman in the lobby who wishes to speak to you. I believe he's a reporter," the man responded.

August shrugged his shoulders. "Don't know what he'd want to talk to me about, but let's go. I'll be right back."

Rita felt almost relieved that her father had something else to do. She had really wanted to talk to her mother in private. Closing the door behind her father, Rita went back to the table.

"I'm glad we'll have a few minutes alone," Rita said, as she took the seat vacated by her father.

"You are?" Beth questioned in surprise.

Rita nodded. "I wanted to ask you to forgive the way I've treated you all these years. I know I was wrong and only acting on hurt and bitter feelings. It was wrong and, despite the fact that you never really wanted me, it wasn't fair to punish you the way I did."

Beth looked as though the wind had been knocked from her. She sat with an expression of complete shock on her face. "What makes you say that I never wanted you?"

Rita felt the tears well in her eyes. "I overheard you. You told my sister that I was such a difficult child to get close to and figured it was your punishment. I heard you say that you never expected to have another child and, in fact, never wanted another child."

Silence hung between the two women as Beth tried to rein in her emotions. "It's true I never planned to have another child after your brother, Edgar. He was, after all, nine years old when you were born." Tears streamed down Beth's face. "I wish I could explain those words. No, I wish I could take them back," Beth whispered.

Rita ached at the sight her mother's brokenness. In the past, she'd thought on more than one occasion of throwing her mother's words in her face. Somehow, Rita thought it would offer satisfaction or compensation for the pain her mother had caused. Now, it just offered Rita grief and sorrow.

Rita started to speak, but Beth waved her off. "Please, let me finish," she said. "I need to tell you all of it."

Rita nodded and sat back waiting for her mother to speak.

"I planned to finally spend time with your father," Beth began. "I hoped to dog sled with him or to at least have more time to just be alone with him. We'd never known a time in our marriage when there weren't children and, after twenty-some years of marriage, I intended to get to know him better as a man and husband, rather than a father.

"I found out I was pregnant after thinking that I was going through the change. Mind you, I was happy to be going through the change. My days of having babies were through as far as I was concerned. So, just when I had resigned myself to move into another stage of womanhood, I found that nothing had changed at all. I was pregnant after a nine-year break and it was devastating."

Rita tried to hide the hurt she felt, but she couldn't. Her eyes betrayed her misery and Beth suddenly realized why all those years had been lost between mother and daughter.

"The story doesn't stop there, however," Beth continued. "I hadn't realized how much I'd distanced myself from you until one day your oldest sister was remarking on the crescent-shaped birthmark you had on your upper thigh. It was like a slap in the face. You were a year old and I didn't even realize you had a birthmark. Suddenly, I started to understand that I'd pretty much given you over to your sisters. They saw you as a chore and not a new baby to play with. They fed you, made clothes for you, changed you, and I surrounded myself in the pretense that I was busy with one project or another and that the experience was good for them.

"Little by little you worked your way into my heart," Beth said with a sad smile. "I found myself watching you. You were such a good baby. So quiet and content. I never had to listen to you fuss and you were never sick. By the time you were a toddler and then old enough for school, I'd come to love you quite dearly. But, the damage, of course, was done. You and I hardly knew each other. For the rest of your life, try as I might, I could never say the right thing or do enough to make it up to you. You never gave me an inch and I can't really blame you. I didn't deserve an inch." Beth fell silent, trying to determine just how she would say what needed to be said.

Rita cried openly and remembered the lonely little girl who longed for a mother's comfort and instead found disinterested siblings at her side.

"I am so sorry, Rita," Beth sobbed. "I don't deserve for you to forgive me, but I love you so much and I can only beg for you to give me the mercy that I didn't show you."

Rita moved her chair back and stood up. Holding her arms out, she whimpered like a tiny, hurt child, "Momma, I love you!"

Beth threw herself into the arms of her child. The years of pain were cast aside as if they were old, useless coats in springtime warmth. The two women cried long and hard in each other's embrace. Fearful of letting go. Not wanting the moment to pass.

When their tears subsided, Rita was the first to speak.

"I could never understand what I'd done so wrong that no one loved me or wanted me around. I used to lie in bed and one minute, I would think of horrible, awful things that I wanted to happen so that I would have my revenge. And the next minute, I'd push it all aside, knowing that I'd gladly give anything I owned to feel loved by you."

"How you must have suffered," Beth whispered. "I can never take that back. I can never make it up to you."

"You don't have to," Rita said, feeling the weight of her misery lifted. "I know now that if I forgive you, then I must let go of the past. That little girl is grown now and we have a future together. Dad told me that his only real worry about leaving this world was that you and I would be alone. Now we can be there for each other. We can start all over."

Beth took hold of her daughter's hands. "I'd like that, Rita. I'd like a chance to put the ugliness aside and start fresh."

"Then that's what we'll do," Rita said and embraced her mother again.

Neither of the women heard August when he returned. When they pulled away laughing, he was there by the door with tears in his eyes.

"Daddy!" Rita exclaimed and held her arms open to him.

August crossed the room, hugging both Beth and Rita to him. "Dare I hope that this means you two have put aside the past?"

"Better than that," Beth replied. "We finally understand the past between us and we're going to forgive it and forget it. Aren't we, Rita?" She looked into her daughter's dark eyes. Eyes so much like her father's that Beth never failed to see August when she saw Rita.

Rita smiled. "We sure are. We have a lot of lost time to make up for."

"Does that mean you'll move back home?" August asked.

"I don't know. I want to get on with my nursing career, but I've come to realize after being home this last year that I don't belong here in Anchorage. I think I'd like to settle down in Tok for awhile. Of course, it will all depend on finding a job."

"I'm sure you could work for one of the local doctors," August suggested. "We'd love to have you back home and, that way, you and your mom could spend more time together."

"Mom isn't my only concern," Rita said gravely.

"What is it, Rita?" Beth asked in a worried tone.

Rita pulled away from her parents and went back to the table where she slumped into the chair. "It's Mark."

"What about him?" her parents asked in unison.

"I don't know where to begin," Rita said honestly.

August sat on the bed, while Beth joined her daughter at the table. "Just tell us what's wrong," August said.

"I'd love to," Rita admitted. "But I'm not exactly sure what really is wrong."

"Is Mark the reason you don't want to move home?" Beth questioned.

"Yes and no," Rita replied. "Mark told me he loved me and asked me to marry him."

Beth and August exchanged a smile. They thought Mark would make a fine choice for their daughter and didn't hide their obvious pleasure.

"How do you feel about Mark?" Beth asked.

"That's my real dilemma. I know I love him. I just don't know that I'm ready to get married. Allowing people to get close to me is something I'm not very good at. I'm not sure I could do justice to Mark's love." Rita's voice was shaky as she continued. "I guess I'm afraid."

Beth reached out and patted Rita's hand. "Committing yourself in marriage is something you should be very sure of. I will tell you this much, however. Most everyone is afraid of the magnitude of marriage."

"What am I suppose to do then?" Rita questioned. "I mean, I do love him and I don't want to lose him—"

"Why not give Mark credit," August interjected. "He

knows his own heart and he's a good solid thinker. Why not share your apprehension with him and take it one step at a time. I have a feeling Mark will know how to handle the situation."

Rita raised her eyes to her father. "Do you think he will think less of me for my confusion?"

"I don't think it's possible for Mark to think less of you," August answered with a laugh. "He's got it bad for you, Rita. I think if you told him to walk to the moon and back, he'd do it."

"But don't take advantage of him," Beth added. "He's a good man and he deserves to be dealt with in an honest manner. Just talk to him, Rita. If you still have any doubts, work through them and take your time. And Rita," Beth paused almost fearful of her next suggestion. "Pray about it. Spend a great deal of time in prayer and I will, too."

Rita nodded. "Of course," she whispered. "I should have thought of that, first thing. Trusting God is something else new to me. I guess I have a lot to learn."

"Don't worry," August said. "God understands all of that and He'll guide you through. Just trust Him for direction, Rita, and when you're afraid, trust Him even more."

Rita couldn't help but smile. "Mark told me about the verse in Psalm Fifty-six that says 'What time I am afraid, I will trust in thee.' It seems like a most appropriate verse for me."

seventeen

Rita stayed with friends in Anchorage until May. She felt that she needed the time away from everyone in order to sort through her conflicting emotions. She had mailed Mark a brief, but poignant letter that offered no promises, but allowed a glimpse of her true feelings for him.

She mostly spent the time in prayer and searching, however. She had determined that it would be foolish to move to Tok without a job. Because of that, Rita gave it over to God and mailed her resume to all of the area doctors in the small town.

"If God wants me in Tok," Rita had proclaimed, "He will provide me the means to support myself."

When a job offer came at the end of April, Rita was nearly stunned from her answered prayer.

"It was what I prayed for," Rita admitted to her mother on the telephone. "I guess I'm still so new at this that I didn't really expect an answer."

"Well, I have another answer for you," Beth replied. "Your father has built a small cabin for you about fifteen minutes away. It's closer to Tok than our place, but close enough to home that you could just hike over if you were of a mind to."

Rita shook her head. It seemed fairly obvious that God wanted her in Tok. "That would make it just under thirty minutes into town," she surmised.

"That's true," Beth answered. "If you don't mind, we'll start fixing it up for you. You know, a few touches of home.

We can take over your old bedroom stuff and put in some new touches as well."

"I don't know what to say, Mom."

"Just say yes, and we'll all get to work." Beth's words were Rita's final straw. She knew God's destiny for her would take her north.

"Yes," she replied into the telephone receiver. "I'll take the train to Fairbanks when the tracks are open for the tourist season. That will be May fifteenth. Can you meet me?"

"You bet," Beth replied, not hiding the joy in her voice. That left only one unspoken problem. Mark.

As if interpreting the silence, Beth braved a question. "Do you want me to tell Mark that you're coming home?"

Rita started to say no and then changed her mind. It would be fairer to warn Mark of her impending arrival. "Yes," she said softly. "Tell him my plans. I don't know that he cares anymore. I sent him only one letter, and he never wrote back. But, I'd still feel better if he knew."

"I understand, and I will let him know." Her mother's words offered a bit of solace.

"Mother?" Rita questioned. "Do you think he still cares for me?"

"Do you want him to?" Beth asked.

After a difficult pause, Rita spoke. "Yes, I do. I really want him to still love me."

"Then give it over to God," Beth suggested, "and trust Him for the rest."

"You're right of course," Rita murmured. "It's really a matter of trust."

☙

Rita was glad for the long train ride home. The miles offered her twelve hours of contemplation time before she would arrive in Fairbanks. For most of the trip, Rita rode the train in the area between cars. She opened the upper portion of the door and allowed the chilled May air to assault her face. The cold felt good and the fresh air seemed to clear her mind.

As the scenery rushed past her, Rita found herself praying. "God, You know my heart even when I don't. This time, I feel that I truly love Mark, but I don't know if he still feels the same way about me or not. Father, I know I must leave this matter to You. Help me not to take it back and work it for my own will, rather than Yours. Amen."

The ride lasted from eight in the morning until eight at night, passing through miles of Denali National Park. It even afforded Rita a picturesque glimpse of Mt. McKinley before the clouds moved in and sheltered the summit from view.

From time to time the forest gave way to glimpses of small towns. Railroads always seemed to approach towns from the backside, Rita decided. It appeared to be just the opposite of the highway on which she'd driven north, a year earlier.

When she caught sight of the DEW line, America's Defense Early Warning system in case of Soviet attack, Rita knew that she was nearly to Fairbanks. She mentally calculated the plans from there. They would no doubt stay overnight, given her parents' dislike of traveling the highways after dark. That would make it at least noon tomorrow before she'd actually make it home. How much longer after that before she could see Mark and talk to him?

When the train pulled into the station, Rita put her concerns of Mark aside and rushed to greet her parents.

"I'm so glad to see you both," Rita exclaimed, throwing herself into their arms. "It's good to be home."

"Well, nearly home," August laughed. "You don't mind

staying over tonight, do you?"

Rita laughed. "No, I already had that planned. Did you get the things I sent by air express?"

"They're safe and sound in your new cabin," August replied.

"My new cabin," Rita repeated. "It seems so strange to know that I'm now a homeowner."

Beth laughed and gave Rita a squeeze. "You're going to love it. I just know it. You should have seen the way your father and Mark worked to finish it."

"Mark helped?" Rita questioned. Was that an air of hope for something more, in her tone?

"Mark nearly built it himself," August answered honestly. "I can't move like I used to. Gerald came over and he and his older boys offered a hand as well. It was a real family affair once your mother started adding the homey touches."

"Well, well." Rita's tone made her pleasure evident. "It's going to be hard to stay over, knowing all that awaits me."

"It'll be just like Christmas," August said with a smile. "You'll have to wait until morning to unwrap your gifts."

"Like Christmas, eh?" Rita questioned teasingly. "Then we can get started at four o'clock in the morning, right?"

August and Beth rolled their eyes. "Some things never change with kids," August laughed. "Come on, we'd better get you fed and to bed, if you plan to get started that early!"

❧

Rita didn't get her parents up at four. She relished the soft mattress of the hotel bed and lingered there until her mother announced that they were going down for breakfast without Rita, if she didn't get around.

She could hardly sit through breakfast, while thoughts of

Mark pressed her to hurry. When they were finally headed home, she couldn't help but count the landmarks and towns. Minutes seemed to drag by, while Rita barely heard the things her parents had to say.

By the time August finally pulled down the dirt road that led to the Eriksson homestead, Rita was gripping the door handle in anticipation. Home had never looked so good to her.

"I drew you a map," August said, coming to a stop beside Rita's car. "I know you want to head right over, but you could stay a spell."

"That's true," Beth added, getting out of the car. "I'd be happy to fix you lunch and—"

"Thanks anyway," Rita interrupted.

Beth and August laughed. "Go on then," August said. He put his arm around Beth and, for the very first time, Rita felt the warmth of the love they shared. She'd once questioned what her father could have possibly seen in her mother. Now, however, Rita thought she was coming to understand.

Rita glanced around, wondering if Mark was working with the dogs. Beth read her daughter's mind and shook her head.

"He's not here, Rita. He's getting your dogs settled at the new place."

Now Rita was even more motivated to see her new home. "I'll see you later," she grinned and jumped into her car.

"Don't speed," August called out to his daughter. "Remember where that got you before."

"I do," Rita said, remembering it fondly. "It found me the man I intend to marry!"

August shook his head and waved her on. It was good to know that his youngest had finally found happiness. Better yet to know that she'd finally found peace of heart and soul.

❧

Rita glanced only briefly at the map. From her father and mother's earlier description and directions, she knew without the paper, just where she was going. She crowded the speed limit as closely as she dared and finally found her turnoff just as her patience was wearing thin.

The dust sprayed out behind her car, as Rita moved closer to her cabin. She rounded the final bend to face a huge banner with bright yellow letters, strung across the road. As she approached the cabin, she found that banners were flying everywhere. WELCOME HOME, they read.

Across the front porch of the huge cabin, another banner in multiple colors, reiterated the message. Rita felt her heart pound faster. Were the banners her parents' idea or Mark's?

Parking the car, Rita got out and stopped. She looked around her, just trying to take it all in for a moment. The clearing set out before her held not only the cabin, but a partially finished shed. From behind the house, Rita could hear the dogs raising a ruckus. They knew their mistress was finally home.

She searched the area for some sign of Mark's motorcycle or truck. Surely he hadn't tended the dogs and left. If he had, did that mean he no longer cared for Rita in the way he once had?

Rita felt a gripping despair come over her. Maybe her anticipated homecoming wasn't what she'd hoped for. Maybe Mark's kindness and work had been done out of his partnership status with her father. Maybe Mark wouldn't want to see her. After all, he'd never even acknowledged her letter.

Rita swallowed hard. Whatever happened was in God's hands. She had to trust Him and count on Him to make the way for her life. Breathing a little easier, Rita stepped forward to explore her new home.

She hadn't taken more than two steps when the unmistakable sound of a screen door opening, caught her ear. Looking up, Rita found Mark coming out from the cabin. He walked to the edge of the porch and stood at the top step.

Rita stopped and appraised him for a moment. His expression was masked from revealing whether their reunion was a welcomed one or something that he was merely tolerating. His brown eyes were serious and Rita felt their warmth as his gaze penetrated her fears.

The wind in the trees broke her concentration and Rita turned momentarily. She looked back quickly, half expecting Mark to have moved or done something that would indicate how he felt. Instead, he said nothing, did nothing. What did it mean?

eighteen

Mark's words came back to haunt Rita. She remembered in Nome when he told her, "Some day you'll come to me and I'll be there with open arms just for you."

Here I am, Rita thought to herself. *Now where is the open-armed welcome that he promised?*

Mark had played his game long enough. When a grin spread across his face, he couldn't help but fulfill his promise to Rita.

Rita ran across the yard and up the steps to where Mark's open arms waited. "I've missed you so much!" she exclaimed as his arms tightened around her.

"You have no idea how hard it was for me to leave you in Anchorage and wait here," Mark replied. "Thought you might have even headed off for Texas."

"I was afraid you wouldn't care anymore," Rita said, lifting her face to Mark's. She needed to see in his eyes that her fears were unfounded.

"I told you that I'm a very patient man," Mark whispered. "Although you very nearly made me a liar. It's a good thing your dad had this cabin project in mind, or I'd have never been able to get through the weeks."

"Oh, Mark," Rita said, burying her face against his chest. "I love you and I'm so sorry for making you wait so long to hear me say it."

Mark pressed his lips to the top of Rita's head. Kissing her hair, he whispered. "The wait was worth it. All things in God's timing are worth waiting for."

Rita released Mark and stepped back. "The loneliness was incredible. I thought of you constantly and all I could imagine was that my foolishness had put you out of reach forever. I was truly afraid that I'd lost my dreams of happiness."

"You're the only dream that has ever mattered, Rita," Mark said with a grin. "And let me tell you, my time up here alone has given me an awful lot of time to perfect that dream."

Rita found Mark's sense of humor contagious. "I did some dreaming of my own," she admitted. "About a tall, broad-chested law officer, who saved my life and stole my heart. You've always been a part of my dreams, Mark. And you always will be."

"Then you'll marry me?" Mark asked for the second time.

Rita stepped forward and put her arms around his neck. "I would be most happy to marry you, Mr. Williams. Positively delighted!"

"Promise?" he said, raising a questioning brow. "You aren't going to change your mind and replace me with another Iditarod dream, are you?"

Rita laughed out loud. "Not hardly, Mr. Williams. You are caught, hook, line, and harness. No Texas or race or cowboys or frozen wilderness is gonna stop me. You're stuck with me, like it or not."

"I like it," Mark said, lowering his lips to Rita's. "I like it very much." He kissed her tenderly while Rita melted against him.

When he lifted his lips, Rita sighed. "I'm going to like this, too. I can tell."

Mark surprised her by taking her hand and pulling her with him to sit on the porch step. "This is going to be new for both of us. We've both been used to independence and

we've both lived our lives without real concern for the decisions we make. Now, however, we'll have to consider
each other in every choice we make."

Rita nodded. "It won't be easy to change our lifestyles
overnight."

"We'll no doubt have our moments, when we're not very
happy with one another," Mark added.

"True," Rita replied. "But if we're honest with each other
and careful to work through those times, maybe we won't
have to spend too much time in strife."

"It's going to be a lot of work," Mark stated.

"You sound like you did when you were training me for
the Iditarod." Rita couldn't help but laugh. She saw the
amusement in Mark's eyes.

"Marriage is going to be even more work than the race,"
Mark answered. "And a whole lot more dangerous."

Rita questioned his words. "Just what do you mean?"

"I hear you don't cook too well," he laughed. "I might
be in for some strange cuisine. Then there's mending and
sewing."

"Whoa!" Rita called out. "I'm a nurse, remember? I
have a job that I hope to do and I enjoy working in medi-
cine. You have the kennel and the dogs. I don't see any
reason why we can't work together and trade off on the
cooking and cleaning."

Mark rubbed his chin thoughtfully. "All right," he said
in a teasing tone. "I suppose that's fair enough. But, I draw
the line at mending clothes. I'm no good at it. I can mend
harness and rigs with the best of them, but I can't even sew
on a button."

Rita laughed. "Me neither. I can stitch up wounds, though.
Does that count?"

Mark put his arm around her. "Maybe your mom could

sew on the buttons."

"Maybe," Rita mused, "she could give us sewing lessons."

They fell silent, enjoying the brilliant sun and the warmth that filtered down to thaw the earth.

"What about dog sledding?" Mark asked suddenly.

"What about it?" Rita questioned.

"You plan to race anymore?" Mark's question took Rita by surprise.

"It all depends," Rita replied.

"On what?" Mark asked her. Now he held the puzzled look.

"On you," Rita grinned.

"Me? What are you talking about?"

"You asked me back in Nome, 'What makes you think I'll let you come next year?' "

Mark laughed and squeezed Rita's shoulders. "I guess I did at that. But, seriously, do you want to race again?"

Rita nodded. "I thought it was wonderful. It was everything I dreamed it would be."

"You suppose marriage will be the same way?" Mark's question caused Rita to think.

"I know it will, Mark. It's the best of all possible dreams and even my goal of racing the Iditarod will never be as great as the goal of making you a good wife."

"You'll be a good wife, Texas Rita." Mark said, dropping his arm to take her hand. "There may be other Iditarod dreams, there may even be other races, but there is only one you—"

"And one you," Rita interjected.

"And together, we'll make the dream a reality," Mark whispered. "With God, we'll work to make a good life together. A life founded on Him."

Rita covered Mark's hand with her free one. Maybe it wasn't such a bad thing to give yourself over to another person, after all. Especially when that other person was God's very best answer to all your fondest dreams.

A Letter To Our Readers

Dear Reader:

In order that we might better contribute to your reading enjoyment, we would appreciate your taking a few minutes to respond to the following questions. When completed, please return to the following:

Rebecca Germany, Editor
Heartsong Presents
P.O. Box 719
Uhrichsville, Ohio 44683

1. Did you enjoy reading *Iditarod Dream*?
   ☐ Very much. I would like to see more books
      by this author!
   ☐ Moderately
      I would have enjoyed it more if _____

   _____

2. Are you a member of *Heartsong Presents*? Yes   No
   If no, where did you purchase this book? _____

   _____

3. What influenced your decision to purchase this
   book? (Check those that apply.)

   ☐ Cover   ☐ Back cover copy
   ☐ Title   ☐ Friends
   ☐ Publicity   ☐ Other _____

4. On a scale from 1 (poor) to 10 (superior), please rate the following elements.

    ___Heroine   ___Plot

    ___Hero   ___Inspirational theme

    ___Setting   ___Secondary characters

5. What settings would you like to see covered in *Heartsong Presents* books?

    _____

    _____

6. What are some inspirational themes you would like to see treated in future books?_____

    _____

    _____

7. Would you be interested in reading other *Heartsong Presents* titles?   ❏ Yes   ❏ No

8. Please check your age range:
  ❏ Under 18   ❏ 18-24   ❏ 25-34
  ❏ 35-45   ❏ 46-55   ❏ Over 55

9. How many hours per week do you read? _____

Name _____

Occupation _____

Address _____

City _____ State _____ Zip _____

Janelle Jamison

THE ALASKA TRILOGY

___*A Light in the Window*—Julie Eriksson returns to the Alaska territory to begin her career as a public health nurse. Her loneliness and discomfort is compounded by Sam Curtiss who persists in proposing a marriage that Julie fears would end her career. HP56 $2.95

___*Destiny's Road*—Beth Hogan has returned to Alaska a widow and mother of two young boys only to find her village overrun by builders of the Alcan Highway. Beth and her sons grow to love newcomer August Eriksson, but Beth knows she can never marry a man who is fighting God. HP71 $2.95

___*Iditarod Dream*—Mark Williams hopes to become more than Rita Eriksson's coach for the famed Iditarod race, but the walls that Rita has built around herself are too strong for human penetration. HP93 $2.95

....Hearts ♥ ong ....

Any 12
*Heartsong
Presents* titles
for only
$26.95 *

CONTEMPORARY ROMANCE IS CHEAPER BY THE DOZEN!

Buy any assortment of twelve *Heartsong Presents* titles and save 25% off of the already discounted price of $2.95 each!

plus $1.00 shipping and handling per order and sales tax where applicable.

HEARTSONG PRESENTS TITLES AVAILABLE NOW:

__HP 3 RESTORE THE JOY, *Sara Mitchell*
__HP 4 REFLECTIONS OF THE HEART, *Sally Laity*
__HP 5 THIS TREMBLING CUP, *Marlene Chase*
__HP 6 THE OTHER SIDE OF SILENCE, *Marlene Chase*
__HP 9 HEARTSTRINGS, *Irene B. Brand*
__HP10 SONG OF LAUGHTER, *Lauraine Snelling*
__HP13 PASSAGE OF THE HEART, *Kjersti Hoff Baez*
__HP14 A MATTER OF CHOICE, *Susannah Hayden*
__HP17 LLAMA LADY, *VeraLee Wiggins*
__HP18 ESCORT HOMEWARD, *Eileen M. Berger*
__HP21 GENTLE PERSUASION, *Veda Boyd Jones*
__HP22 INDY GIRL, *Brenda Bancroft*
__HP25 REBAR, *Mary Carpenter Reid*
__HP26 MOUNTAIN HOUSE, *Mary Louise Colln*
__HP29 FROM THE HEART, *Sara Mitchell*
__HP30 A LOVE MEANT TO BE, *Brenda Bancroft*
__HP33 SWEET SHELTER, *VeraLee Wiggins*
__HP34 UNDER A TEXAS SKY, *Veda Boyd Jones*
__HP37 DRUMS OF SHELOMOH, *Yvonne Lehman*
__HP38 A PLACE TO CALL HOME, *Eileen M. Berger*
__HP41 FIELDS OF SWEET CONTENT, *Norma Jean Lutz*
__HP42 SEARCH FOR TOMORROW, *Mary Hawkins*
__HP45 DESIGN FOR LOVE, *Janet Gortsema*
__HP46 THE GOVERNOR'S DAUGHTER, *Veda Boyd Jones*
__HP49 YESTERDAY'S TOMORROWS, *Linda Herring*
__HP50 DANCE IN THE DISTANCE, *Kjersti Hoff Baez*
__HP53 MIDNIGHT MUSIC, *Janelle Burnham*
__HP54 HOME TO HER HEART, *Lena Nelson Dooley*

(If ordering from this page, please remember to include it with the order form.)